W9-AWK-695

THE SAVER'S

GUIDE

TO SOUND

INVESTMENTS

David M. Brownstone

A GROLIER COMPANY

FRANKLIN WATTS
NEW YORK   LONDON   TORONTO   SYDNEY

Library of Congress Cataloging in Publication Data
Brownstone, David M.
The saver's guide to sound investments.
Includes index.
1. Investments—Handbooks, manuals, etc. I. Title.
HG4527.B685 1985   332.6'78   84-20904
ISBN 0-531-09589-4

This publication contains the author's opinion on the subject. It must be noted that neither the publisher nor the author is engaged in rendering investment, legal, tax, accounting, or similar professional services. While investment, legal, tax and accounting issues in this book have been checked with sources believed to be reliable, some material may be affected by changes in the laws or in the interpretations of such laws since the manuscript for this book was completed. Therefore, the accuracy and completeness of such information and the opinions based thereon are not and cannot be guaranteed. In addition, state or local tax laws or procedural rules may have a material impact on the recommendations made by the author, and the strategies outlined in this book may not necessarily be suitable in every case. If legal, accounting, tax, investment, or other expert advice is required, one should obtain the services of a competent practitioner. The publisher and author hereby specifically disclaim any personal liability for loss or risk incurred as a consequence of the advice or information presented in this book.

PREFACE

This book aims to supply small savers and investors with some useful information and some even more useful insight. The information it contains relates to the wide and often bewildering range of new and old savings and investment tools and techniques now available and being sold hard all over the country by banking, brokerage, mutual fund, and insurance people. The insights it offers have to do with the savings and investment choices that individuals must make, which have such lifelong importance.

I have tried to write about these sometimes complex matters simply and clearly. In truth, there is nothing so very difficult about the matters discussed here, once you begin to understand some of the special language of these fields and recognize that much of what seems complex is really just financial selling talk. We can understand money and its uses, and that understanding can help make us free.

My thanks to Irene Franck, whose insights as always illuminate and improve every aspect of my work; to Jacques Sartisky, for his clear-eyed view of all matters financial; to Gene Hawes, for endless hours of fruitful discussion;

to our excellent typists, Shirley Fenn, Nancy Fishelberg, and Mary Racette; and last, but far from least, to William Newton of Franklin Watts, the editor of this work, who did so much to help shape it.

David Brownstone
Chappaqua, New York

CONTENTS

THE SAVER'S
GUIDE
TO SOUND
INVESTMENTS

CHAPTER 1

What You Need to Know About Saving and Investing

This is a book for the small saver and investor, the kind of person who has every right to feel pretty good about coming out of any year a few thousand dollars ahead, and who may have a nest egg for savings and investment measured in thousands and tens of thousands of dollars, but not in hundreds of thousands or millions of dollars. The very well-to-do heart specialist, corporate executive, or business owner should look for advice from high-paid investment advisers, accountants, and lawyers, who will focus on tax-advantaged investments. The overwhelming majority of small savers and investors have very different needs, and those needs are the focus of this book.

Every once in a while—not often, just every once in a while—the main opportunities available to small savers and investors change. Not the pitfalls; they remain regrettably much the same, though under different names, from year to year and decade to decade. But new opportunities do emerge, in our time usually because the federal government decides to attempt to control the American economy a little differently, or to encourage savings and investment a little differently, or just to give in to the demands of one or another pressure group. Yes,

we know about free enterprise and the American dream
and the evils of government control—but the fact is that
*small savers and investors are now in a brand new and
much better ballgame* because the government has
  • *deregulated the amount of interest that federally in-
    sured banks can pay savers.*

The high federally insured interest rates now available provide *a new standard* aganst which all other savings and investment must be measured.
  • *made new laws that allow people to build up their
    own tax-deferred retirement accounts.*

These accounts grow very quickly, as have corporate
retirement plan monies over the years.
  • *managed the economy—as much as it is able to do
    so—so as to make interest available to small savers
    and investors at a higher rate of return than the rate
    of inflation.*

This last has probably also caused a good deal of
unemployment and is surely creating deficit problems
that will haunt us and our children and grandchildren
for generations—but the fact is that right now the interest
you can earn is much higher than the rate of inflation.

How those three factors work together to your advantage, in specific savings and investment forms, is much
of the content of this book. The key understanding at the
start has to be that the situation has indeed changed
greatly for these three reasons—and so much for the
better that, for the first time since the boom years of the
1960s, it really pays people to economize, save, and invest. In that way, even with all the other problems facing
us as individuals and as a people, these are years of great
opportunity. We cannot know how long that will last; for
now it is so and to be taken advantage of if at all possible.

It also absolutely must be said that some things in the world of savings and investment hardly change at all. As always, there are some investment "professionals" around who will urge you to gamble—even with your retirement money—on speculative stocks, sometimes masquerading as "aggressive growth" mutual funds, on sometimes worthless municipal bonds, on high-risk real estate, and on bad business deals mislabeled tax shelters. Some will even take you into such extraordinarily foolish gambles as stock options and financial and commodities futures. Many will help you compound your troubles by making it easy for you to borrow money, often through the device of the margin account—shades of 1929 and the late 1960s! There are also a good many investment books around that will tell you how to get rich quick— there always are.

An enormous number of absolutely innocent lambs are talking quite knowingly about the joys of "leverage," without having the slightest notion of what leverage is all about: that it can take you up fast but take you down much faster, and always at the wrong time, with the slide down being pushed by several then-out-of-control factors. And a distressingly large number of new and old investment professionals are very cheerily fleecing both a new generation of obliging lambs and a substantial number of people who have been through all this before and should know better.

This book then is essentially a consumer's guide for savers and investors, covering a wide and often bewildering range of old and new opportunities and pitfalls. It is as simple and basic as I can make it, for that kind of writing and treatment is what I think the vast majority of savers and investors desperately need in this new period.

THE RANGE OF SAVINGS
AND INVESTMENT CHOICES

There aren't really very many basic savings and investment choices—though there are a good many ways of organizing those few basic vehicles, usually for selling purposes. When you have ten different brands of cornflakes, and they are all essentially the same, you have to spend a good deal of time and money extolling yours as unique and supremely satisfying. When you have ten— or fifty—big banks selling the same kinds of savings accounts, or one hundred securities firms selling the same kinds of mutual funds, you get a lot of different sales names and an enormous amount of often confusing sales talk. Fast talk, too. The municipals seller who calls you to urge purchase of a very high-yielding bond is unlikely to tell you also that the bond yields so much only because it is thought by professionals to be very risky. And the conservative bank officer who sells so many IRAs (Individual Retirement Accounts) is unlikely to tell you that one bank's IRAs are likely to be virtually indistinguishable from another bank's IRAs—and that he or she is selling IRAs hard in order to win a trip to Hawaii in the bank's sales contest.

Here are the main basic savings and investment choices. They will be discussed one by one in coming chapters, but it can help a good deal to have them all laid out together at the start, for purposes of quick comparison.

• *You can put your money into a bank.*

You can, in effect, lend your money to a bank; the bank will relend your money, making its profit on the difference between what it pays you in interest and what it gets in interest from its customers. After all the talk about new kinds of accounts, full service, bank relations, social responsibility, and the new financial marketplace, that is still what banking is all about from the banker's viewpoint.

Your loan to the bank can be in the form of one of several kinds of *demand deposits*, meaning that you can get your money back out any time on demand. Or you can lend it in the form of *time deposits*, in which you can get a somewhat higher rate of interest in return for tying up your money for a specified period, anywhere from a few months to many years. Whatever else they may be called, for the bank's selling purposes, all accounts are either demand or time deposits.

With deregulation—meaning that banks can now pay you whatever rate of interest they see fit, instead of being limited by law as before—*some federally insured demand and time accounts are superb for small savers and investors*, especially when used to fund Individual Retirement Accounts (IRAs) and Keogh plan accounts, which are greatly tax-advantaged. But some bank accounts held by millions of people are no better than they were before and should not be held now at all. Some bank accounts are also not properly insured, and some kinds of bank-issued investment vehicles might, to the unwary, seem to be insured but are in reality not insured at all. And within the wide range of basically good new accounts now being offered, some are much better than others in general, while some are better for particular purposes. All of these questions need to be discussed in detail and form much of the substance of this book.

- *You can lend your money to other public and private borrowers, buying their bonds and notes.*

When you buy a federal, state, local, corporate, or

other public or private bond or note, you are lending your money to the issuer of this debt obligation. The rate of interest is usually stated as firm throughout the term of the obligation, and that term can run anywhere from a few days to as long as several decades. If you hold the bond or note to the end of its term, you get your money back, and have either had interest at stated intervals during the term of the obligation or get a larger lump sum at the end. Before the end of its term, you may have a hard or easy time selling the bond—and you may sell it for more or less than its stated value. Both matters depend on the nature of the bond: on who issues and guarantees its payment, and on the fluctuations in the general interest rate between the time you buy it and the time you want to sell.

In uncertain times—and these are *very* uncertain times—it is unwise to tie your money up for very long. And it is extremely unwise to lump all kinds of government and major corporate bonds together, considering them all relatively safe investments. Some short-term federal bonds are excellent for small savers and investors, being as safe as any investment can be and in some periods yielding excellent rates of return. But many longer-term federal bonds may decline in value and hurt you considerably, even though they are safe (that is, you will not lose the amount you invested). So may many corporate bonds—and many of these may not be so very safe, either. And so may very many state and local— generally called municipal—bonds; although tax-advantaged, these may not be at all safe, as a good deal of recent experience so clearly indicates. We will be discussing the several kinds of bonds and their safety and interest factors—as well as the selling talk that accompanies so many of them.

• *You can buy stock.*

Buying stock is buying a share in a company. It should in no way be confused with buying a bond, which is lending money to a company. When you buy shares, no one owes you anything in the way of dividends or interest, except that some kinds of stock have to pay stated dividends before other kinds of stock can receive any. Even if the company whose stock you buy has an excellent dividend-paying record, it may stop such payments at any time, with no penalty to the company except perhaps a decline in the price of its stock—which hurts you as stockholder just as much as, and perhaps more than, it hurts the company.

When buying stock remember that you are sharing ownership risks and rewards, and that each stock represents a unique company and must be understood in terms of potential risk and reward. We will discuss common stock, preferred stock, relatively—but only relatively—safe stocks, the nature and hazards involved in speculation, the virtue of sharing ownership in a company you know and regard highly—especially if you work for such a company—and a good deal more in relation to stock investment.

• *You can buy shares in mutual funds.*

When you buy a share in a mutual fund, you are giving your money to someone else to invest for you, usually on the theory that investment professionals pooling large funds can invest more effectively than you can, even though you will have to pay something for having those professionals handle your money.

Mutual funds come in as many varieties as there are investment instruments and investment goals. There are stock funds, corporate bond funds, municipal bond funds, money market funds, balanced funds, income funds, growth and aggressive growth funds, and a good many more. There are also thousands of mutual fund sellers, many of them capable, others ready to tell you whatever you want to hear and sell you whatever you want to buy— or whatever they have to sell.

With those thousands of sellers can sometimes come some very large sales charges, taken off the top of your invested money. Such charges are to be avoided; they have nothing at all to do with the quality of the investment management offered by the various mutual funds, as a smallish separate management fee is always charged. We will discuss the main kinds of mutual funds available and some of the very substantial pitfalls involved in mutual funds investing.

• *You can put some of your money into tax-advantaged Individual Retirement Accounts (IRAs) or Keogh plans.* For small investors and savers who can somehow manage each year to put away at least a little money that need not be touched until much later in life—and doing so is really a must—*IRAs and Keoghs are the best investments in the world.*

You can invest through your IRA or Keogh plan in any or all of the kinds of savings and investment vehicles previously discussed. You can manage your funds yourself or have professionals manage them for you for a fee. Up to specified yearly amounts, your investments are wholly deducted from your income for income tax purposes, and you are not taxed on the growth of your money until you start withdrawing funds from the account, which can be as late as age seventy and a half and as early as age fifty-nine and a half.

There are pitfalls here, too, having to do with guaranteeing the safety of your later-years and retirement money. A good many people—often encouraged by investment professionals who should and sometimes do know better—are speculating with their retirement money, usually without having the slightest idea that they are doing so. But with adequate safeguards against speculation, these can be wonderful ways of developing large later-years funds, and should be for each of us an enormous incentive to save and invest. And when available interest rates are considerably higher than the rate of inflation, the adventages are greatly magnified, for reasons we will detail later in our main discussion.

- *You can buy life insurance with savings and investment features.*

When you buy an annuity policy, you are, in essence, putting your money into the hands of an insurance company, which will usually charge you sales and management fees, and take some portion of the profit from the money invested. On the other hand, it will guarantee a fixed payout at a specified time, if you wish. When you buy a life insurance policy with "cash surrender value," you are similarly putting part of the premiums you pay into the hands of the insurance company for investment. Millions of people buy both of these kinds of insurance policies every year. Our discussion of such policies will deal with them as ways of saving and investing, rather than with their insurance aspects.

- *You can invest in real estate.*

Small savers and investors may improve their own homes, directly purchase other property that has been built upon or improved, or buy raw land for long-term investment purposes. You may invest in residential or commercial property—as a sole purchaser, in full partnership with others, or only as an investing "limited" partner. We will discuss the several ways of investing in real estate and the opportunities and hazards accompanying them. All too often, real estate investing is seen too much from its tax shelter aspects and not enough as a straightforward investment matter. And all too often, small savers investing in real estate listen too uncritically to those who tell them how to use leverage to make millions in real estate—and wind up going broke instead.

• *You can buy gold, silver, gems, collectibles, and other such hard goods.*

In the mid-1980s, the bloom is off many of these kinds of investments, which were so popular in the depression-fearing, inflation-ridden mid-1970s. But they are not entirely to be counted out, even in this period, as a troubled, deficit-ridden American economy—and a world economy in even deeper trouble—will provide ample cause for continuing worry. Some small savers and investors will still want to put part of their money into such investments; all should have a sufficient understanding of what they really are and how they work as investments, and should be able to take money in and out of them, as demanded by the times and by their own fears and needs.

• *You can speculate.*

The hard goods above can be hedges against depression and inflation. They can also be handled as high-risk, potentially high-yielding speculations, and often are. Add to them such purely speculative investments as stock options (unless they are in your own company), commodities futures, and financial futures, and you have a pretty substantial number of ways to lose your shirt. We will discuss these kinds of investments, but mainly in a cautionary way, as we believe that small savers and investors have no business at all risking their precious savings on speculations.

This book deals with making money with your money

in direct ways that can easily be measured and compared with each other. It does not cover some other sound but hard-to-measure of using savings. One such is using your savings to go into your own business; another is the use of savings to pay for education of yourself and others, which so often results in far greater incomes than would otherwise have been possible and in satisfying lifelong careers as well. Such investments are sometimes the most profitable, however, and should be considered in any investor's wider personal planning.

SOME BASIC QUESTIONS TO ASK ABOUT EACH SAVINGS AND INVESTMENT CHOICE

Making good decisions on money matters—and on most other matters, as well—depends largely upon learning the right questions and consistently asking them about each money move you make. It has to be done consciously at first, sometimes for years; but after a while, asking the right questions becomes the most valuable reflex you possess. Here are some key questions to ask yourself every time you are considering a savings or investment move:

• *What is the risk?*
Yes, risk first, not reward. It is all too easy to be seduced by potentially high rates of return and lose sight of basic risks. This is not to say that you should take no risks—or that for small sums you should not sometimes even risk losing all you put in. *The key thing is to understand the risks* and then rationally decide to go into or stay out of an investment. The small investor who

tries to become a high flyer by speculating in commodities futures with a few hundred dollars is not much different from someone who goes to Las Vegas and puts the money into slot machines—and the results are very nearly as predictable. No catastrophe, though. The catastrophe is when a small investor puts all of his or her IRA retirement money into an aggressive growth fund, doesn't bother to watch the progress of the fund carefully enough, and suddenly finds that the fund has lost half its assets in a protracted market downturn. Or when you put your savings in an uninsured bank, even though you could have put the money in a federally insured bank that paid the same high rate of interest. Or when you put your money into a single-premium deferred annuity, paying interest that seemed at the time too good to be true—and lost most of your money because it was *indeed* too good to be true.

But risk does not always—or even nearly always—involve potential catastrophe. Most risks must be measured against potential rewards. You may get a sure 9 percent interest on your money in a federally insured, bank money market account that is entirely liquid—meaning that you can get your money out easily. But if you can get 12 percent on a well-rated bond issued by a strong corporation, you may go for the corporate bond—as long as you figure you won't need to pull the money back out soon or suddenly. In that case, you might have to sell the bond itself at a loss, which would negate the higher interest rate you had been receiving—and then some. And if you compare that safe 9 percent with buying a common stock that last year yielded its holders a combination of 15 percent in dividends and growth in the market value (price) of the stock, you might decide to buy the stock—but only if you think the stock will continue to do well and recognize that the stock may go down a great deal, as well as up.

On the other hand, you may be someone who is very worried about the future of the American economy and decide to put a good deal of your stake into gold, reasoning that it is the safest possible kind of investment. In a way it is, in that it is likely to hold much of its value in good times and grow in relative value in bad times. But in a way it isn't and must be seen as carrying its own very real risks. For gold pays no interest, and it tends to lose value in good, confident times—losing its value doubly then, because inflation eats away at the value of the dollar. So safety is not always so very safe, and the question of relative risk is never a simple one, except as regards such hopelessly risky speculations as futures and options. That, by the way, is why this book contains no neat little risk-reward table for the various kinds of savings and investment vehicles. I have never seen or created one that made enough sense to be really useful to small savers and investors. I prefer to discuss risks and rewards separately for each kind of choice.

• *What is the reward?*

That's really two questions. One is *"How much will I make?"* That can be applied to savings and investments yielding fixed, clearly stated rates of interest, such as the bank deposit above. The second is *"How much might I make?"* The answer to that question always has some "ifs" and "maybes" in it. The stock discussed above may yield you 3 percent in dividends and 12 percent in market price growth next year, for a total of 15 percent, as it did this year—but neither is guaranteed. It could yield you the same 3 percent in dividends, lose 12 percent in market price, and yield you a minus 9 percent by the time you grimly decide to sell it at a loss. If you had bought it on borrowed money, as with a margin account loan from a broker, your gain or loss on invested dollars would be larger—with leverage working both ways, as it always does.

Reward is properly seen as *yield* and *net after-tax yield*, at that. "Yield" is the amount of money you will make on your money, usually expressed as a percentage of the amount of money you have committed. For example, $200 put into a bank certificate of deposit with a total yearly yield of $20 after all the bank charges and compoundings of interest, has yielded 10 percent. "Net after-tax yield" is that $20, or 10 percent, minus taxes, if any, on the money you made. If you were in combined federal, state, and perhaps local income tax brackets that caused you to pay 30 percent in the top bracket of your taxable income, then your net after-tax yield would be $20 minus $6, for a net of $14, or 7 percent.

In real life, figuring net after-tax yield is not as easy as in this very simple example. There are tax wrinkles that favor some kinds of savings and investments over others. There are also estimates to be made, as to what your gains on some kinds of investments might be, such as the stock purchases and bond sales earlier discussed. And there are estimates as to what your top tax brackets will be, which depend partly on what successful and legal tax avoidance moves you are able to make.

The main thing is to learn how to make soberly reasonable estimates of possible risk and possible reward for each main savings and investment decision, weighing each against the other, while properly identifying and avoiding possible catastrophes.

• *Have I figured in the taxes?*

The discussion of net after-tax yield above makes it clear that there is always the tax question to be considered.

For people with large incomes, the tax questions are always vitally important, but smaller-income people must always take taxes into account, too.

In the example above, a 10 percent yield on savings before taxes becomes a 7 percent net after-tax yield. Perhaps that does not sound like much, but in reality it is, once you add a few zeroes and spin out the difference over a number of years. An average of $10,000 in an IRA or Keogh account, compounding monthly at a full tax-deferred 10 percent over a period of thirty years will grow to be almost twenty times its size, to $198,374. But the same $10,000, growing at 7 percent for thirty years will grow much less, to $81,165. Both are very large amounts, well illustrating the desirability of doing some saving, but the 10 percent—over thirty years—yields almost two and a half times as much as the 7 percent.

While we're doing some figures, let us also point out that if you can manage to put just $1,000 a year in an IRA for thirty years, and interest rates hold in at least the 9–10 percent area, you are quite likely to wind up with somewhere around $150,000 in that IRA account at the end of those thirty years. We are now and may be for some time in a period in which interest rates available are greater than the inflation rate, so that $150,000 may really mean something by retirement time—and not just be eaten up by inflation.

- *How fast and at what cost can I get my money out if I want or need to do so?*

This raises the rather standard question of *liquidity*. Cash, or what you can very easily convert into cash at full current value, is liquid. A bank demand deposit, for example, is liquid, as are federal debt obligations. Widely traded stocks, bonds, and mutual funds are easily salable, but perhaps a little less liquid, because you may have to take a loss on a quick sale, if a lot of other people are selling at the same time. Hard goods like gold, silver, and gems are the classic liquid investments, considered capable of being turned into cash even when national currencies may be worthless—but if you have to sell them at a bad time, you may also have to take a big loss. Savings and investments with a time element, like time deposits and tax-advantaged retirement accounts, usually have substantial penalties attached for early cashing in; they may be salable, but they are illiquid to the extent of those penalties. And some items may under some circumstances be quite illiquid, as when you cannot sell real estate or a business when you want to, even though you may be willing to take a substantial loss. You must consider liquidity—that you may want or need to get your money out—when making any savings and investment decision.

- *Am I making this savings or investment decision on the basis of my own informed judgment?*

In the long run, this is the most important question of all, underlying all the other questions and all the other saving and investing do's and don'ts. Putting it a little differently, it is absurd and wrong to make any savings or investment decision without knowing exactly what you are doing and why. Outlining all the tools and techniques of lifetime personal financial planning is beyond the modest scope of this book (though I have done that before in other books which are as near as the nearest substantial public library). But it still must be said here that there is no substitute for developing a set of lifetime financial plans, keeping as informed as possible, finding long-term financial advisers, and investing only in what you know or can come to know through careful study.

Here is a list of rather basic savings and investment

do's and don'ts, based in large part upon the need to develop your own informed judgments, while resisting and at the same time learning from those who would sell you on the merits of their particular savings and investment tools and techniques.

DO'S AND DON'TS

This section might well have been called Don'ts and Do's, for there are a good many more ways to go wrong in the financial world than there are to go right. That is especially true for small savers and investors, who do not have the resources and advice available to larger investors. Generally, where the large investor may sometimes choose to gamble, the small investor should not. For example, where someone with high income can cushion losses on bad tax-sheltered investments with tax savings, the small investor usually cannot.

For small savers and investors, maximizing savings and investment income involves buying as inexpensively as possible and with the smallest possible continuing service charges. It also involves skepticism, patience, continuing self-education—and of course always asking the right questions.

Do set up your own tax-deferred retirement plan, no matter how small at the start, and add to it regularly. Individual Retirement Accounts (IRAs) and Keogh plans are by far the best investments available for small savers and investors; not to set them up is gross negligence.

DON'T gamble with retirement money. Whether you have others handle your plan or direct it entirely by yourself,

be very sure that your retirement money is invested conservatively. Especially avoid temporarily high-flying
common stocks that can come down faster than they went
up and aggressive growth mutual funds that are composed
of essentially the same kinds of stocks.

DON'T depend upon company pension plans or Social
Security payments to take care of your financial needs in
your later years—and don't believe those who tell you
it will somehow be all right in the end. That is nonsense.
We live in extraordinarily troubled times and will see
many more seemingly very stable companies—and their
pension plans—fail in the decades to come. And we live
in deficit-ridden times. We will see a continuing assault
on the real value of Social Security payments all our lives
and a constant tendency to reduce pensioners to life at
a bare subsistence level, if that.

Your modest IRA or Keogh funds may very well be
the difference between living out your later years com-
fortably and fruitfully, and living them in poverty and
despair.

DO make a lifelong habit of always asking the right questions about every projected savings or investment move,
making a serious attempt each time to balance potential
risk against potential reward, taking into account safety,
liquidity, and net after-tax yield.

DON'T "take a little flyer this time, just this once." Little
flyers can turn into big ones, with a little success at the
start turning into a larger and larger commitment, complete with big profits—on paper—and an eventual disaster. And just about the worst thing that can happen to
you is to make some money on a speculation early in an

investing career, develop the unspoken, entirely erro-
neous, but very real idea that you are somehow able to
outguess everyone else, and form the habit of "a little"
speculation.

DON'T put your money into anything on faith, on trust,
on whim, on hunch, on a tip, or on any of the other
utterly misleading emotional bases that every day cause
people to lose money unnecessarily.

That also means that when your stockbroker calls
you with something "really hot," you should not buy—
even if the last five really hot buying suggestions from
the same stockbroker have made money for other people,
and even if you know those people and are sure the money
was made. On the one hand, you can usually be pretty
sure that you are hearing only about the winners and
from the winners. On the other, backing what may be
only a series of lucky guesses is no better than betting on
someone who is having a streak of lucky passes at a Las
Vegas crap table; lucky streaks end.

Sellers—of anything, including savings and investments—should also be viewed skeptically, no matter how
much you like and respect them as individuals. A salesperson sells what he or she has to sell, even though many
financial industry firms are now carefully cultivating the
image of the "financial supermarket." For example you
cannot expect a banker to tell you that another bank
nearby is offering a higher rate of interest or that his or
her own bank's charges are higher than those of competing banks. You cannot expect a stockbroker to tell you
to move your long-term funds into federally insured certificates of deposit (CDs), though that may be the right
thing to do at a particular time, or to inform you that
the brokerage firm's money funds are neither as safely

insured nor as high-paying as a bank's CDs. Be a rational buyer, keeping your wits about you and your skepticism intact at all times.

Do save and invest in specific savings instruments and specific companies, governments, and other institutions, or in mutual fund portfolios, rather than in "the market," in gold, in real estate, or in some other general kind of investment. Outside of investing in mutual funds, you won't have enough money to diversify meaningfully— that is, to spread your savings and investments over many risks—so you would not be able to ride with a particular market even if you thought that desirable. If you do choose to diversify by investing in one or more mutual funds, be very sure that you know and understand which stocks or debt obligations they are holding and that you want to hold those investments as if you had bought them yourself.

Don't invest in a market, or a kind of industry, or a kind of investment. Consider your particular investment on its own individual merits. That the Dow Jones industrial average has been going up—which is what most people mean when they say "the market has been going up"— means far less than that you have invested your money in a sound, relatively stable company. That you are "pretty heavily into the computer industry" may mean that you are holding some very good IBM stock—or that you are holding the stock of some very troubled smaller computer companies, in the process of being destroyed by IBM's marketing power, new foreign competition, and market glut. That you are "into municipal bonds" may mean that you have been buying and holding some bonds issued by relatively strong state and local governments, that have been forced by adverse market conditions to pay quite high interest rates to get money, and that you are therefore receiving both high interest and tax advantage, adding up to very high after-tax yield at moderate risk. On the other hand, you may be "into" state nuclear energy power bonds, or you may have bought the bonds of a one-industry town in which that one industry has just closed down. In either case, you may be holding defaulted-on bonds worth about 15 cents on the dollar—if you can find anyone to take them off your hands. Buy on the specifics.

Do buy from people you know, though after you get to know them, much of your business may be transacted by telephone and mail. No matter how small a saver and investor you are, anyone reputable in the financial industry will welcome your visit and show you around the office, usually joyfully discussing far more than you really want or need to know, about everything from the way the telephone system works to how hard it is to get good help nowadays. People love to talk about their businesses; financial people are no exception to that rule.

Don't buy from anyone who discourages that kind of office visit or who will not show you around a little. Even though federal and state governments are quite vigilant, there is still a good deal of fraud out there. And along the same lines, *don't buy anything from strangers over the phone.* A truly astonishing number of people still do that, buying everything from phony stocks and bonds to substandard or nonexistent "gems" in sealed containers that "can't be opened or you breach the guarantee." Yes, the gem swindle actually happened; so did the sale of nonexistent gold bullion that the seller was kind enough to hold in his own vault and which the people who "bought" it never even saw. Those swindles were exposed, with resulting prosecutions, but only after a large number of small investors had lost millions of dollars. Where there is money, there are thieves; be careful.

Do buy stocks or bonds through a discount broker or through the discount brokerage operation of a bank. In recent years, a national network of discount brokers has developed, with commission schedules far lower than those of standard stockbrokers. And very recently, many banks have begun offering discount brokerage services, as well. At this writing, many smallish discount brokerage transactions are being made at about half the prices charged by standard brokers, and as new competitors enter the field, prices will continue to go down.

Don't buy stocks and bonds through high-priced stockbrokers on the theory—pushed hard by the high-priced firms—that by doing so you will get the benefit of their research and investment counseling. It is illogical to expect them to be able to do that for you on the kind of volume a small investor provides; there just isn't enough money in it for them. At most, you will get a newsletter and some printed recommendations, and perhaps a call from a salesperson once in a long while, trying to sell you something. If you want to keep informed—and you should—use the money you save on high-priced brokerage transactions to buy a subscription to the *Wall Street Journal*—and read it.

Do consider the question of tax shelter—that is, the shielding of income from taxation—as an important element of your savings and investment thinking. As we have seen, a soundly invested tax-sheltered IRA or Keogh plan can accumulate far faster than the same amount of money at the same rate of interest in nontax-sheltered investments. And a relatively high-interest tax-sheltered municipal bond can yield more net after-tax income than can many higher-paying corporate bonds—although you must be very careful as to the safety of municipal bonds. There are many quite sound tax-sheltered investments in these areas and in such investment areas as real estate and the exploitation of natural resources.

DON'T put your money into an investment mainly because it is tax-sheltered. For some very high-income investors, tax-shelter aspects may be as important as whether or not the investment itself is sound, but for small investors the investment must *first of all be a sound one*, although enhanced by its tax-sheltered aspects.

DO take advantage of federal policy, which protects deposits in federally insured banks by insuring them up to $100,000 per account. All other things being equal, it is far better to have your money protected by federal insurance than by the kind of private insurance available from some money market mutual funds; in a real financial crisis the mutual fund insurance may fail, while the federal insurance will probably hold up as long as there is a federal government with the ability to raise money through taxes and to enforce its laws. Should a new situation cause money market mutual funds to pay significantly better yields than bank money market or similar funds, then by all means consider going to the mutual funds, as long as their insurance continues to be reasonably well funded through major insurance companies doing business in your state.

DON'T put your money into a banking institution that is not insured by the federal government. There are still a few that aren't insured at all; when they go under, as some do, their depositors may lose all or much of their money. There are many more that are insured only by their state governments. They have been safe until now, but you cannot count on that safety to continue indefinitely, as many states face very serious and growing financial problems. It costs nothing at all to be very prudent here; keep your bank money in federally insured accounts.

DO keep informed as to general savings and investment trends, and DO be very sure to read the prospectus on each proposed new offering very carefully. Pay special attention to all the *cautions* that offerers are forced by law and regulatory authorities to put into their prospectuses. Take what is said in warning in a prospectus very seriously and literally, and pay no attention at all to the investment seller who, by tone and shrug, indicates that you should not pay much attention to "all that stuff." The seller can't really say anything like that directly without violating the law, but there are lots of ways to indicate that you really should ignore the warnings plainly placed into the prospectus.

DON'T invest in a new offering until you have very thoroughly read and are sure you understand the offering as explained in the prospectus. If you have questions, ask them of the offerer, and if the answers are not satisfactory, don't invest—no matter how good it all looks otherwise, no matter how strongly the investment is recommended by others. Many small investors are entirely put off by the difficult, often evasive, and ambiguous legal language

of many prospectuses but invest anyway, on the recommendations of investment sellers and friends. Don't
do that; lambs follow.

DO watch your savings and investments very carefully.
Move in and out of them as the situation demands, even
though that may mean selling out and taking a loss.

DON'T hold onto a losing investment out of sheer pride
and stubbornness, as it goes down. The hallmark of the
amateur investor is that he or she comes into a rising
market or buys a rising investment rather late and at or
near highest prices, and then holds the investment far
too long, while the investment goes down, unwilling to
take the loss.

DON'T ever act on the theory that a particular savings or
investment vehicle is as "safe as the Rock of Gibraltar"
and need not be carefully watched over the years. There
never was any such place to put your money, and there
certainly isn't now. Yesterday's blue-chip investment or
safe municipal is today's failed or obsolete company or
bankrupt municipality. Nothing is that safe, even United
States government obligations. An unfortunate time may
come when it will make more sense to put your money
into gold and survival supplies than into federal debt
obligations. Many governments in our time have drasti-
cally devalued currencies, for example, and bankrupted
many small savers and investors. It hasn't happened in
the United States, but it might, and it is wise to be alert
to that kind of possibility.

DO pay close attention to the service charges, management fees, and sales charges imposed by banks, securities

firms, mutual funds, insurance companies, and all others who handle your money. You have every reason to be a comparative shopper among financial organizations; such charges vary widely, often with no relationship at all to the quantity or quality of services actually rendered.

DON'T pay heavy sales charges unless you feel that the financial offering or services rendered are so far superior to comparable offerings or services that you absolutely must buy. Some mutual funds, insurance companies, and real estate syndicators will charge you as much as 9 percent right off the top of your money for their own selling costs, most of the money going directly to the people who have sold you the fund or insurance policy. This is called *front loading*. That means that, at the moment you buy, your saved or invested dollar has become worth 91 cents and that if you wanted to pull your money out the next day you would have lost 9 cents on each dollar. It also usually means that you have not comparative-shopped hard enough or have bought the wrong kind of instrument. Perfectly good *no-load* mutual funds of every kind are available; you need not pay front-load charges. Similarly, perfectly good term insurance policies are available on a no-load basis, as well as many of the more expensive insurance policies with cash surrender valued included. Because front-loaded policies are preferred by many insurance agents and brokers, no-load policies may be a little harder to find, but they are worth searching for.

CHAPTER 2

The New
High-Interest
Bank Accounts

For small savers and investors, the bank account game has changed very greatly in the last few years. As federal banking laws have changed, partly because of new policies aimed at stimulating savings and investment, and partly because of successful financial lobby pressures, much more favorable interest rates and deposit arrangements have become available. *The result has been the creation of a whole new group of federally insured high-interest-paying bank accounts, into which you can put both short-term and long-term money with small minimum deposits, and which set a new standard against which all other savings and investments must now be measured.*

What has happened is that the country's banks, which have been very highly regulated since so many failed during the early years of the Great Depression, have in recent years become largely deregulated. In addition to this, we have been in a period of higher interest rates than any other period in this century—indeed, so high that long-standing usury laws limiting the rates of interest lenders could charge have been repealed throughout the country. The net effect is that banks are active in a lot more kinds of financial businesses than they have been at any time since before the Depression, and that the interest rates they are charging their borrowing customers are so high that they can afford to pay very high rates of interest on the money you lend to them.

What all this will do to the country is not clear. Bankers, as a group, are notorious gamblers with other people's money, contrary to the image so carefully cultivated by the industry. The latest evidence of that is the recent worldwide lending spree, in which American, Western European, and Japanese bankers have lent well over $600 billion to countries that clearly are not going to pay back more than a small fraction of the money—money that we will wind up paying, one way or another. That is why it does not do to be lulled into a false sense of security at any time. There is a chance in these years to make good money on your deposits in federally insured bank accounts, but I am in no way saying that you can now put your money into a bank, forget it, and just watch it grow. Far from it. You should watch your bank account investments just as carefully as you watch any other investments; stand ready to move them as quickly as necessary, and hold a little cash and some valuables out of the banking system at all times. One of the most important lessons to learn from the difficult times of the last decade or so is that the United States is not immune to the kinds of economic problems that beset other countries. We learned that lesson last during the Great Depression and tended to forget it during the good years of the postwar era and the boom years of the sixties, but should have relearned it by now.

This is a period of transition from old savings and investment arrangements to new ones. As a result, there is a good deal of quite understandable confusion about what kinds of accounts are available, what they really pay, and which are most desirable for what purposes. Those questions are further complicated by the strenuous selling efforts of the nation's bankers, brokers, insurers, and other financial industry people. There seem to be several overlapping kinds of accounts, a multiplicity of possible banking services, and a truly bewildering array of interest rates, compoundings, penalties, service charges, management fees, yields, effective yields, savings periods, and "bargain" special offers. In short, a pretty wide open financial marketplace is developing out there, with a lot of financial people selling hard to tens of millions of small savers and investors. Banks are not banks anymore; they are "financial supermarkets," just as stockbrokers are no longer simply stockbrokers, but rather "complete financial planners." That is all very well, but small savers have to understand what is being offered, what it costs, what it yields, and how to comparison-shop.

BANK ACCOUNTS

As used throughout this book, "bank" means a commercial bank, savings bank, savings and loan association, or credit union. Most bank deposits have, since the 1930s, been insured by several federal and state agencies. The Federal Deposit Insurance Corporation (FDIC) insures deposits in most commercial and savings banks. The Federal Savings and Loan Insurance Corporation (FSLIC) insures savings and loan association deposits. The National Credit Union Association (NCUA) insures credit union deposits. All insure up to $100,000 per account in a single bank, as of this writing; you can hold as many separate insured accounts in as many banks as you wish, so there is no effective ceiling on the insurance available. IRA bank accounts are insured separately, so you can actually hold $200,000 personally in a single bank. Also, a married couple can hold up to $200,000 in a single bank and still be insured. Many states also insure deposits, but be sure that your accounts are covered by federal deposit insurance. And remember: Some banks have no insurance at all. Make sure your bank is not one of them.

Whatever they are called for selling purposes, there are still only two basic kinds of bank accounts, the *demand deposit* and the *time deposit*. A demand deposit is money you have put into a bank account that you can reclaim at any time, without notice to the bank—that is, on demand. A time deposit is money you have put into a bank account that you are, in effect, lending to the bank for a specified period of time; you either cannot get that deposit back until the end of that period, or— as is more usual—you can get it back earlier only if you give up some of the interest you would have earned on the money.

A small *caution* on demand deposits: They may not always be there when you demand your money, even though they may be covered by federal insurance. Since the Depression, federal insurance has picked up swiftly after specific bank failures, and people have been able to get at their deposited money quickly. And even in a major banking system collapse—which could happen, and don't let anybody convince you that it could not—you are likely to get your federally insured money eventually. But only *eventually*. That is the situation in which demand deposits may not be available on demand, and a little cash and valuables kept out of the banking system may prove very useful.

A second *caution*, on the way *compound interest* is figured. Compound interest, being essentially interest figured on top of previous interest, builds your money a good deal faster if it is figured daily than if it is figured in any other way. For example, if you have a dollar in the bank at a 10 percent yearly interest rate, and that dollar has its interest added to it once a year, you will get only the stated 10 percent per year. But if that interest is figured daily, the resulting interest on top of interest will give you a yearly interest of nearly 11 percent. That is what is meant by the *effective rate of interest*, so prominently featured in all the bank ads. The more frequent the calculation of interest on top of interest, the better it is for you: Quarterly is better than yearly, monthly is better than quarterly, and daily compounding is best of all. Many banks have developed ways to cut the interest they pay while seeming to pay you stated rates, such as compounding monthly and paying you only on the lowest balance showing during the month, or handling withdrawals so that you get interest for shorter periods than you are really entitled to. There are new tricks developing all the time; find and stick with banks that straightforwardly compound your interest daily, with no tricks.

There are new selling hooks developing all the time, too. The main recent *caution* here regarding the new bank accounts is around *offered interest rates*. When a bank offers a wonderful 14.3 percent on your money, when all others are offering 9–9.5 percent, look for the fine print: You will usually find it right on the newspaper ad, in very small and often almost illegible print somewhere underneath the big numbers of the offer. When you read it carefully, you will find that the wonderful interest rate is being offered for only somewhere between a week and two months, depending on when in the advertising campaign you happen to see it. Be careful. The kinds of bankers that run that kind of potentially deceptive come-on—and some very big banks have done so—are also likely to have figured out some pretty clever ways of getting their money back.

It is also wise for the small saver and investor to resist participation in the financial supermarket approach now being taken for marketing purposes by banks and other financial organizations. In the long run, it is far better for your financial health to think of bank accounts as *service or convenience accounts* and *investment accounts*.

A *regular or special checking account* is essentially such a service account. In some circumstances the unused money in these accounts, hooked up with small savings accounts, can pay modest interest that will partly offset the cost of the bank's check-handling services, but interest opportunities are rather small. Aside from that, no interest is paid on such deposits. You will probably choose these kinds of accounts more for physical convenience than for the few dollars you can make or save on check handling and related interest arrangements, even though many banks spend a lot of time and money touting their services and savings for small depositors in these areas.

Similarly, a *passbook savings account,* a *statement savings account* (which only means no passbook is issued), and a savings account with check-issuing privileges included for a fee, such as a NOW *(negotiated order of withdrawal)* account, should all be treated as convenience accounts. They all pay terribly small rates of interest, from 5¼ to 6 percent on your money in a period when equally safe accounts pay much higher rates of interest. No one should keep savings in such a low-paying account when the same money can be put into an entirely liquid bank money market account at much higher interest. Unfortunately, millions of small savers still have their money in such accounts, to their loss and their banks' great gain. *Always bear in mind that because of the way compound interests works, a few extra percentage points yearly can triple or quadruple your money over the course of twenty to thirty years of consistent saving.* The differences between one bank's service accounts and another's will make little long-term investment difference to you. When deciding where to place your service accounts, choose the bank that is most convenient physically or some reasonably convenient bank that seems to offer a little more service or somewhat smaller charges. All other things being equal, you may even choose the bank whose statement is easiest to read and understand. These are very small matters.

But do not let where you keep your service accounts greatly affect your choice of where to place your investment accounts. For those, comparative shopping is very much in order, along with a continuous review of investment choices and the kind of money moving and handling that you cannot possibly do with convenience bank accounts, because of the sheer bother involved.

BANK LIQUID MONEY MARKET ACCOUNTS

One of the most popular accounts in this period—and for good reason—is the high-interest demand deposit bank investment account usually called a *money market account*. The name stems not from what it is and is invested in, but because it was developed in competition with money market mutual funds, which in the late 1970s and early 1980s competed successfully with banks for investment funds.

In fact, the bank money market account is a bank savings account that pays whatever rate of interest the bank chooses to place on it, usually varying from week to week, and which may be withdrawn on demand. The interest rates offered will depend partly upon such money market factors as the rates being paid by the federal government on its own debt obligations, but mostly on how much the bank is able to charge those to whom it lends money. That, in turn, depends on many factors, including the kinds of borrowers the bank mostly lends money to, the bank's other costs, and the kinds of bad debts the bank is carrying—as from that foolish lending spree abroad. At this writing, there is a great difference between what banks are paying depositors for lending the banks money and what the banks are charging for money. Indeed, it is the greatest such difference in modern times. That is one of the two main reasons why banks are paying what seem such high rates for getting deposits, the other being the general very high interest rate level in the economy, which has much to do with government deficits and government manipulation. With deregulation, banks now have a great deal of leeway as to what interest rates they can pay, with much depending upon their guesses as to whether interest rates are likely to rise or fall in the years ahead and by how much.

When legal interest rate ceilings on bank accounts were deregulated in 1983, banks all over the country— and especially in New York and California—competitively paid interest rates in the 12–14 percent yearly range (but only for a month or two) to attract new customers with their money market accounts. Within a few months, interest rates paid on these accounts had dropped sharply, into the 8–10 percent area, and they were then paying about as much as money market mutual funds.

The best thing about the bank money market fund is that they are federally insured up to $100,000. Many money market mutual funds have made private insurance arrangements in an attempt to enhance their safe image as part of their battle with the bank money market funds, but private insurance may not be able to cover these accounts in the sort of crisis that would cause many such mutual funds to go under. Other money market mutual funds are invested wholly in federal government obligations and are in that sense entirely safe, but may because of those investments pay somewhat less than their bank and mutual fund competitors.

There are drawbacks connected with the bank money market funds, though. One substantial drawback is that many charge fees unless a minimum balance, such as $500, is maintained. Even a seemingly small charge, such as $2.50 a month, can take away from interest earnings significantly in that sort of situation, negating the value of the bank fund for very small accounts. An investment of $600 in a money market fund at an "effective rate" of 10 percent in a year yields only $60. A $2.50 per month fee becomes $30 a year, or half of the interest, with the effective rate of interest then becoming only 5 percent; the account then becomes a mistake to maintain. Similarly, many bank funds pay no interest on any day in which your balance becomes less than $500. It doesn't take many such days to reduce sharply the effective rate of interest on such small accounts.

In contrast, most money market mutual funds need minimum investments to start with, though some are for as little as $500–$1,000, but then require that no minimum balances be maintained. There are sometimes very modest management fees, but these are not stated as part of the effective rate of return. There are no monthly fees or tricks with minimum balances and interest payments.

For small amounts, then, the money market mutual funds seem much superior to most bank money market funds. For larger amounts, it becomes a matter of watching the interest rates being paid by each, keeping the very small risk factor in mind, and moving your money to your best advantage. Do keep an eye on that small risk, though. If you have any reason at all to begin worrying about an imminent crash, move your money into federally insured accounts.

Whenever you do move any money into bank liquid money market funds, be very careful to be alert to any charges, adverse ways of figuring interest, or misleading come-on offers. Do not take it for granted that because a bank is large and well known, and has an excellent and conservative reputation, it is above all that. Far from it. On these matters, all banks are to be considered equal— and should be treated with equal skepticism. No seasoned banker will be insulted by your skepticism. Quite the contrary: They will respect you more for it.

CERTIFICATES OF DEPOSIT (CDs)

Time deposits are now generally called *certificates of deposit (CDs)* in banks throughout the country. That can and sometimes does lead to a little confusion about what these kinds of deposits really are, as corporations also issue short-term debt obligations called certificates of deposit, which are likewise based on their bank deposits. But corporate certificates of deposit are issued in large denominations, usually for no less than $100,000, and are negotiable—that is, tradable—because they cannot be cashed in by their holders until their due dates. The time deposits now called certificates of deposit by the nation's banks are issued in much smaller denominations, are usually cashable (though at a penalty) before their due dates, and are therefore nonnegotiable.

The basic transaction involved in the issuance of a CD is that you are lending the bank your money for a specified period of time at a guaranteed rate of interest for that period. You are essentially betting that generally available interest rates will not rise dramatically during that period, which would cause you to lose the money you might have earned in those higher interest rates. The bank is betting that interest rates will not fall dramatically in that period, forcing it to cut the rates it charges on its money while continuing to pay you high rates, and therefore losing money or not making as much as it could. Most banks really are currently betting quite heavily that the general level of interest rates will not go down very much in the next decade; that is why they are offering long-term interest rates as high as, or higher than, those they offer for liquid money market accounts.

You can put your money into a certificate of deposit (CD) for pretty nearly as long or as short a time as you might wish. Not all banks will offer the same choices as to length of time, but competitive pressure will soon ensure that you can very readily secure a CD for a period of anywhere from one month to ten years—as long as interest rates remain relatively stable, that is. When they begin to fluctuate sharply again, then banks will cut the number of long-term options available, or will make them yield such unattractively low rates of interest that few will want to buy the long-term CDs. As of this writing, many banks are offering to tailor-make your CD, usually for periods ranging from a little over one month to five years, but sometimes up to ten-year terms.

For all federal and state insurance purposes, these bank CDs sold to consumers are bank accounts and are therefore insured up to $100,000 for all of your accounts in a single bank, with separate insurance for IRAs, double the amount for married couples, and no ceiling on the number of banks in which you can hold such insured accounts.

The interest you get on money invested in CDs is fully taxable, unless it is sheltered in IRAs or Keogh plans. Even so, safe and fully insured CDs at current high rates of interest are prime investment opportunities for small investors and savers.

One safety feature about CDs that is sometimes not fully understood and appreciated is that they cannot go down in value during their lifetimes. Corporate and municipal bonds can and do; when interest levels go beyond the interest rates being paid by the corporate and municipal bonds you are holding, those bonds tend to lose market value for trading purposes in direct relation to the rise in interest levels. (More on that later, when we discuss bonds.) If you want to get part of your money out of a CD during its life, you may have to borrow against the CD from its bank issuer, and if you want to get all of your money out of a CD before it is due, you may have to pay a substantial interest penalty. But you won't have to sell the CD at a loss in either instance.

At this writing, you can buy a short-term bank CD, maturing in a year or less, for minimum amounts of $1,000, with longer-term CDs carrying $500 minimums. But by the time you read this book, bank minimums around the country will probably have gone down to $250 or even less, to match the competition offered by money market and other mutual funds.

Banks will automatically "roll over" your CDs for you if you wish; that is, at your request, they will reinvest the proceeds, including accured interest, when your CDs mature.

That is a valuable service, and you should instruct them to do that for you. We're not all as well organized as we might wish, and it is very easy to forget that you have a CD maturing as of a particular day. Without an automatic rollover, your CD money will then sit in the bank until you remember, earning nothing for you. If you have linked several kinds of accounts, CD proceeds may be moved into a low-interest-paying savings account, or perhaps a checking account that pays no interest at all, with your then-high balance only serving to fund a few checking transactions.

Many banks and some brokerage firms are now offering *asset management accounts*, in line with their evolution as financial supermarkets. These are accounts set up to handle many kinds of financial transactions within the context of a single unified account and unified statement. In them, banks and brokers will undertake to supply such previously normal banking services as checking and savings, and add to them a wide variety of other services, including a choice of several kinds of CDs and liquid money market accounts, IRA and Keogh plans, discount stock brokerage, the purchase and storage of precious metals, several kinds of credit lines, and several kinds of credit cards. To accomplish all this, they will often contract with other kinds of financial organizations, such as mutual funds, to supply investment services to their clients. Many of these accounts "sweep" available savings and checking funds from lower interest paying service uses into such higher paying uses as money market funds. Not all banks and large brokers offer such services, but the trend is in that direction, and in most substantial cities and suburban areas you will find at least one bank or broker offering such accounts.

There are often minimum-size-of-account limitations that preclude many small investors from seriously considering opening such an account, the most common minimums at this writing being in the $10,000 to $25,000 range. But competition is now beginning to force down minimum account requirements, and small investors with IRAs and Keoghs are in many instances building up personal assets rather quickly. A working couple can put $4,000 a year into IRAs, and in four years with growth have as much as $20,000 in IRAs. Add some CDs from previously accumulated savings, a modest discount brokerage account, and some working cash, and you have far more than you need to open such an account.

For those with enough assets and enough activity to justify paying the charges associated with such accounts, they can be a good idea. They are convenient; being able to call a single source regarding possible statement errors is a very real plus in a world full of statements and printouts, each organized differently. Beyond that convenience, though, they can serve a much more important purpose—that of making continuing sense out of your daily financial life, and thereby enabling you to do sounder lifetime financial planning.

There are charges, though, often in the neighborhood of $50–$100 beyond the customary checking account charges you would otherwise pay. There are also separate charges for such functions as discount brokerage and often also for such matters as Keogh plan administration. And there are charges—often stiff ones, with very high penalties for late payments and defaults—for credit lines. And with charges a *caution*: All of these charges may be perfectly competitive and quite acceptable to you, but it is necessary to understand them and to have comparative-shopped them before opening such an account with anyone. There are often very substantial differences between the asset management accounts of banks and those of brokerage firms, with banks offering more safety and a somewhat wider and more flexible line of services, but with brokerage firms offering lower total charges. But if you have more yearly trades, the high-priced brokerage firm may ultimately cost you far more in total money spent than the bank with discount brokerage facilities. On the other hand, the bank may cost less for brokerage transactions, but you may find yourself paying the bank 2 percent a month and large attorney's fees if you are in default on your bank line of credit, as well as having your securities sold out from under you at a large loss.

These asset management accounts can provide convenience and financial planning help, but I do have considerable concern about your putting all your financial eggs into one basket. Reading the fine print on some agreements required by banks for their asset management accounts makes it clear that there are liabilities: Your funds and securities can be tied up if any of a considerable number of events should occur, and the bank has a good deal of discretion as to how to handle matters if you should get into financial trouble. If you are seriously considering this kind of account, it may be wise to shift your securities trading, especially if it involves borrowed money in margin accounts, to some other agency, rather than mix financial reserves and speculative activities. Similarly, it is wiser to store your valuables, such as gold and negotiable securities, in your own safe deposit box, rather than in a bank account or under bank control.

Beyond such questions as the nature of the basic transaction, government insurance, safety, available terms, and the mechanics of rollovers, you must consider the basic strategic questions of (1) how long you want to tie up your money, (2) at what anticipated or guaranteed rates of return, and (3) in what kinds of investments. These are the three main questions for savers and investors; all the rest, including the consumer cautions we will mention a little later on in this chapter, are matters we will all become increasingly familiar with as we get used to this kind of investment instrument.

Your answers to those three basic questions depend mostly on how you think interest rates are likely to go in the years ahead. Not how you think the economy will go. Interest rates these days are at least as responsive to government manipulation as to economic conditions, and we can have high or low interest rates in a wide range of situations, from depression to modest recovery. That is part of the problem of predicting interest rates; when American internal politics, the views of conflicting economic schools, and out-of-control international conditions all powerfully impact upon interest rate fluctuations, prediction beyond the short term becomes very nearly impossible.

For those reasons—and because I believe that the American economy will, for at least the next several years, move up and down around a stagnant center, with interest rates unsuccessfully manipulated by successive groups of politicians—I urge you to *keep your money short-term*. That is especially so for bonds, which are very likely to fluctuate a good deal; it is also so for CDs. Long-term CDs can cost you a good deal in foregone interest if interest rates go up sharply, and can hinder you in the lifelong battle to do better than the rate of inflation.

By short-term, I mean one year or less. Many financial industry people still think of short-term investments as those of up to three years. That is their training—and that is the way it was until current very uncertain times. When a banker, broker, or financial adviser talks about investing in short-term obligations, be sure that you are both talking about the same thing.

Staying with short-term CDs can mean that you will fail to "lock in" a 10–11 percent rate of interest and have to take much smaller rates of interest in conditions of either deep economic depression or surging prosperity, as in either instance general interest rates are likely to be relatively low. However, in either of those instances you may not want to have a substantial proportion of your money in CDs. In depression, you may very possibly think it wise to shift a good deal of your money into harder stores of value, such as gold and gemstones. In real prosperity, you may want to move a good deal of your money out of debt obligations altogether and into shares, for then many stocks may be excellent investments, at least during the good years. So don't worry too much about "locking in current high rates of interest." That's mostly just financial industry salestalk.

A lot of advertising has been generated around these CDs. Some ads directly solicit CD purchases from banks, while others focus on buying CDs from banks when putting money into Individual Retirement Accounts (IRAs). A good deal of that advertising has been purposefully misleading, though legal requirements have forced publication of most of the facts, often in very small, hard-to-read print.

A *caution* as to offered interest rates is very much in

order here. When you see a bank offering something like 14.3 percent in very large black letters in an ad, when all or most other banks are offering something like 9.5 percent, you can be sure that you are seeing nothing but a come-on. As in the discussion of bank liquid money market funds, the high rate may only apply for a week to two months. But here acceptance is much more damaging; with a CD you cannot pull out when you realize that you have been misled by the ad. An additional 5 percent interest on $2,500 for one month is only about $21. Anyone who tries to mislead you that way on a CD purchase is probably someone you should not be doing business with.

A *caution* also on the terms of the offers. As this is being written, I am looking at a full-page bank ad offering a CD at an annual interest rate about 0.5 percent higher than most other current short-term CD offers. The offer is in very large print. The very small print underneath the numbers indicates that the CD being offered is for *four years* and that the rate offered is therefore only about the same as most other such longer-term CDs at this time. The ad is probably not at all illegal, but it is misleading; it is necessary to comparison shop for CDs.

Many banks are also advertising what they call protection in the event that interest rates go up while you are holding a longer-term CD such as one for two to five years. A *caution* here, too. What they are offering is the option of going over to a variable rate, usually tied to the 91-day Treasury bills rate or some other such index, if interest rates rise beyond the rates being paid on your current long-term CD. That is all very well, but be sure that they also guarantee that interest rates will under no circumstances go *below* current guaranteed rates, once you have gone over to the variable CD. Otherwise, you may find yourself "locked in" all right—to a long-term variable rate CD paying low rates of interest at a time when you could be doing far, far better. Be *very* careful on this one.

A *caution* also on the ability to get your money out of the CD. Be sure that you can get your money out on demand, even though you will have to pay a stated interest penalty for doing so. Back in the mid-1970s, some holders of time deposit accounts were surprised to find that, according to the terms of their agreements, their banks had the option of refusing to let them get their money out of time deposits before their maturity dates.

And finally a *caution* on those penalties. If you may have to use the money from your bank investment account soon, it is far better to put it either into a bank liquid money market account or a money market mutual fund at a fraction of a percent less interest than a short-term CD, than to pay a substantial interest penalty on early termination of the CD. The early withdrawal penalty on a CD of less than one year is likely to be at least one full month's interest, and sometimes more, which may take your interest down by as much as one third to one half of what you should have earned. The early withdrawal penalty on longer-term CDs is often three or four months of interest, and may be even more. That could, under some circumstances, cut your earned interest down to nothing at all.

All cautions having been voiced, it is in order to restate the conviction that these new bank investment accounts are excellent short- and long-term money-making opportunities for small savers and investors, as long as they are comparison shopped, cautiously bought, and watched as carefully as you would watch any other investment.

CHAPTER 3

The Best Investment in the World— If You Handle It Properly

The need to have your own personally controlled and privately funded retirement plan should be painfully obvious by now. All over the country, millions of older people are living in poverty and near-poverty, betrayed by their own illusions about the affluent "golden years" that were going to follow the many decades of hard work— and by generations of leaders who promised social justice and instead delivered Social Security payments that cannot, in the long run, be trusted to pay for anything more than bare subsistence, if that. Corporate pension plan payments that looked pretty good years ago now prove inadequate because of the inflation of the 1970s. Savings that were supposed to be capital and provide interest to live on are instead eaten up and gone all too soon. And we live longer—much, much longer—and therefore have much greater lifetime needs than did those who were here before us.

The truth is that, if you do not take your future into your own hands and build up funds for your later years as consistently and skillfully as you possibly can, you are quite likely to spend your later years painfully poor, with the government and the younger people in the society doing their best to forget you. The plight of millions of older people in this country is something we should all be ashamed of, and it will get much worse before it gets much better, for a whole complex of reasons that are beyond the scope of this book. But know this: They are we. The shabby old man or woman rooting around in a garbage can in a back alley may be you or me some day, if we are somehow unable to take care of our own financial futures.

The government does not provide much—and is in real terms providing less and less as the years go by—but it has managed to pass laws allowing us to develop our own personal retirement plans well, by making available tax breaks that no one should ignore. By using those tax breaks, small savers can now build really meaningful retirement funds from modest, consistent yearly savings, with the money (up to stated limits) exempt from taxes when you put it in and building up tax-free until you take it out. *The difference between building up retirement money with these tax breaks and trying to build it up without can—and probably will—be for many of us the difference between poverty and modest comfort in our later years.*

INDIVIDUAL RETIREMENT ACCOUNTS (IRAs)

For most small savers and investors, setting up an Individual Retirement Account (IRA) is the main way of building a tax-advantaged retirement fund. Even many people in small business for themselves find building an IRA simpler and more in line with the amount of money they can manage to save each year than a Keogh plan—

even though they are eligible to set up a Keogh, which can become much larger, due to higher legal limits on the amount you can save tax-free.

With an IRA, you can take a certain amount out of your earnings each year, treat the amount taken out as a straight deduction on your income tax return, and have these amounts accumulate tax-free in a special retirement account until you start taking money out of that account later in life. It is wise to put money into your IRA every year, whatever your income that year, and particularly beneficial during your peak earnings, high tax-bracket years, for you are likely to be taking money out of it in lower-income, lower-bracket years later in life. The deduction and tax-free accumulation together provide an opportunity to accumulate far more than you possibly could if the money were treated and taxed as ordinary income.

Here is how it works, as of the time this book is being written, in the spring of 1984. You can be quite sure that the rules will change as the years go by, especially as regards higher legal contribution limits.

PUTTING MONEY INTO AN IRA

As an individual wage earner, you can put up to $2,000 of your earned income each year into your Individual Retirement Account (IRA) until the tax year in which you reach the age of seventy and a half. If you are married and your spouse is not working or has no earnings for the calendar year, you can put up to $2,250 of your earned income into a joint IRA with your husband or wife. If you are both working, you can each set up an IRA, so that a married working couple can put up to

$4,000 a year into IRAs. Note that an unmarried couple can do the same, setting aside $2,000 each in separate accounts, as long as both are earning. But the $2,250 contributions ceiling applies only to legally married pairs.

You cannot put in more than you earn, though. You can't, for example, earn $1,000 part-time and put $2,000 into an IRA; your contribution that year would be limited to the $1,000. Earnings can be from any source, but unearned income—including interest, dividends, pensions, and rents—does not qualify.

You don't need to put the maximum amount—or any amount at all—into your IRA each year. Once the IRA has been set up, you can skip yearly contributions if you like. Nor do you need to put your money in just once a year; you can put it in as often as you like, up to the maximum allowable. Also, you can for each year put money in up to the unextended income tax due date, usually April 15, of the following year; that means you can get a very clear view of the amount of taxes you will owe on the previous year's income with and without the IRA contribution. When you see how much you can save on taxes by putting money into an IRA, you will be much encouraged to do so.

Some banks, by the way, advertise that they will lend you money for your IRA contribution, which you can repay in part out of tax refunds. You should approach that proposition very cautiously, as the interest you might have to pay on the borrowed money—although itself tax deductible—might very well cancel out the tax benefit that year from the IRA. It is far better to put less than the maximum into the IRA in a year in which you are short of cash, and put in more in good years. You'll also maximize your tax deduction benefits that way, because your income is likely to be taxed more heavily—that is, you will be taxed in higher brackets in good money-making years than in leaner years. As a general rule, don't pay banks any more interest than you have to, no matter how good the come-ons look or how fancy the tax-avoidance arithmetic.

It is important to recognize that the IRA is not a single investment. Rather, it is a legal structure for sheltering your retirement money from taxes. That money can be invested in a wide variety of ways, though some types of highly speculative investments are prohibited, as we will discuss later. Nor can you simply put your money into an IRA and then forget it—any more than you should do so with any other investment. You may choose to set up a self-directed account, one which you watch on a daily or weekly basis and in which you make all the investment decisions, with or without advice from others. Or you may want to set up a "passive" account, in which you leave the day-to-day investment decisions to a custodian or trustee, such as a bank or other financial institution. With a passive account, you will monitor your IRA on a longer-term basis, assessing changes in the economic, political, or social climate, and comparing your yield at least annually as against other types of potential IRA investments, with an eye toward moving your account for higher net yield, if that seems indicated. Either way there are decisions to be made, and you must watch your IRA and make appropriate modifications in your investment, if the IRA is to fulfill its promise for you.

Note that the money you put into an IRA accumulates tax-free, regardless of how you invest it. Interest, dividends, and capital gains income are not distinguished for tax purposes in an IRA. However the money in your IRA account makes money for you, it will not be taxed until it either begins to be drawn out of the IRA account or is left in longer than allowed by law.

TAKING MONEY OUT OF AN IRA

As the law now stands, your IRA money must be left in your account until you are at least fifty-nine and a half and no older than seventy and a half. You can begin to draw money out as early as fifty-nine and a half without any kind of tax penalty and may keep right on putting money in rather than drawing any out until you are seventy and a half. At seventy and a half, you must begin taking money out, with the amount you must draw out each year depending upon what the actuarial tables indicate your average life span may be as of then. If you had, for example, a twelve-year average anticipated life span at age seventy and a half and an IRA fund of $240,000, you would have to draw one-twelfth of that $240,000, or $20,000, in that year. The next year, with an average anticipated life of eleven years left, you would need to draw one eleventh of the sum remaining plus whatever interest you had earned that year. The penalty for failure to withdraw the minimum sum is 50 percent, of what you should have drawn, but did not.

Any money taken out of an IRA is taxable at regular rates for ordinary income for the tax year in which it is withdrawn. That is why very few people will take out their IRA money all at once in a lump sum, or in a few large yearly payments; it defeats one of the purposes of setting up the IRA. Lump-sum payments will be taxed in much higher brackets, and therefore at much higher rates, than payouts over many years, especially in those later years in which you will be working part-time or not at all, and have special later-years tax deductions, as well. To take large payouts before you must is to cost yourself a great deal of money in tax payments.

PREMATURE WITHDRAWALS

You will also cost yourself money by taking out IRA money too soon. For any money taken out of an IRA before you are fifty-nine and a half, you must pay both ordinary taxes on the payout and a 10 percent penalty on the amount of the money taken out. Only if you have a doctor-certified disability that makes it impossible for you to earn money for a year or more, or have a terminal illness, does the 10 percent penalty for early withdrawals not apply. On the other hand, it is well worth noting that, even if you do have to take money out of an IRA prematurely, the tax-free accumulation of money in that IRA may *still* make it worthwhile to have. The 10 percent penalty on a "premature" IRA takeout may be much less than the difference between the extra money you have earned with an IRA and what you might have earned on after-tax money without an IRA.

For example, if you start an IRA when you are thirty, and put in $1,000 a year for twenty-five years, at 11 percent a year in interest, the $25,000 you will have put in will be worth over $114,000 at the end of those twenty-five years. But the same amount of savings, in a standard account that is not tax-sheltered, may earn only 7 percent after taxes; that would be worth a little more than $63,000, a difference of $51,000. If you had to take out of your IRA $20,000 for pressing personal reasons at age fifty-five, and had to pay both ordinary income tax and penalties on the premature withdrawal amounting to 50 percent of what you took out, you would have cost yourself $10,000 and netted $10,000—and would still have $94,000 in the IRA, continuing to grow tax-free with the rest of your IRA money. In short, you would still be way ahead.

So don't be deterred from setting up an IRA by the thought that, at some time in the future, you may need to take some money out of it prematurely; the advantages are still very great.

ROLLOVERS

IRAs are also good for people who will retire from firms holding corporate pension plans, who have Keogh and deferred-compensation plans that are being terminated by employers, or who have changed jobs. You can set up an Individual Retirement Rollover Account to receive sums due you from those kinds of plans; by doing so you can keep the sums accumulating tax-free and take payments over a long period of time, rather than have to take lump sums and pay high taxes on them in your earlier years.

The talk of rollovers can become a little confusing, though, because there are two other kinds of IRA transactions also often commonly called rollovers. The first of these can occur when you change the custodian of some or all of your IRA money, as when you decide to move some IRA money from a bank to a stock brokerage IRA. Then you write a letter to the old holder of your money, instructing it to move your money to the new custodian. You will often be charged $5–$15 for making that transaction, but you can transfer your IRA account as often as you wish. You can even move your money among several of your IRAs, for there is no limit on the number of IRAs you can set up, only on the total amount of money you put into IRAs in any one year. Or you can set up a new IRA and close out old ones, essentially carrying your money in a single IRA. If you do the latter, be careful not to hold more than $100,000 in a bank IRA, for that is the limit of federal insurance on bank accounts. As you near the insurance ceiling, start new IRAs in other federally insured bank accounts—and be sure that your bank *is* insured, for not all are.

The other kind of rollover transaction occurs when you have a custodian of your IRA money send you all or part of the cash in your IRA account, for reinvestment in another IRA. You can do that only once a year and must reinvest the money in another IRA within sixty days, or have the money be treated, for tax purposes, as a premature withdrawal. In that case, it will be considered ordinary income for the year and also be subject to the 10 percent penalty tax. Some investors have used this kind of once-a-year temporary IRA withdrawal for emergency cash needs, but that kind of use is most unwise. The sixty days pass very quickly, the money to reinvest has been used up, the new money to replace it is slow in coming—and suddenly the period is gone and the penalties apply.

You can also move IRA money, usually at no charge, among several kinds of similar investments within an investment "family" managed by the custodian of a single IRA, as when you move your money several times in a single year among mutual funds managed by a single mutual funds organization.

Physically, it is very easy to set up an IRA. All you

have to do is fill out a very simple form which registers the existence of your account with the organization you choose to be the trustee of your IRA money and start the account with a check, cash, or money order. Many trustees—such as banks, insurance companies, and brokers who have set up the appropriate trusts under the law— will require as little as a $50 opening sum for your IRA account. Many will even fill out the forms for you, doing as much as they can over the phone and by mail. IRA accounts can be extraordinarily lucrative for financial organizations; rest assured that they will make it very, very easy for you to open one. And there are as many kinds of IRA accounts as there are kinds of financial organizations offering them.

As the newspaper ads so clearly indicate, *banks* are prime offerers of IRA accounts. These accounts are essentially savings accounts, offering fixed or variable rates of interest, and they usually are federally insured. Their investment policies are set by the banks themselves. As owner of an IRA account, you are mostly a passive investor here, being active only to the extent of watching rates of return and switching to other banks or to other kinds of investments as you think desirable, as made possible by the nature of the bank deposits you hold. Time deposits carry interest penalties for premature withdrawal, as already discussed; the IRA owner who decides to lock in current bank rates of interest for the long term has also decided not to switch those locked-in savings to other investments, other than in exceptional circumstances. IRA account fees are usually rather small at banks, running from perhaps $15 per year down to no fee at all.

Private *money market mutual funds* are also prime sellers of IRA accounts. So are *standard mutual funds*, offering everything from conservative dividend-oriented investment packages—called portfolios—to the rather speculative aggressive growth portfolios. More on these when we discuss kinds of investments. Mutual fund IRAs, like bank IRAs, are passive as to the individual stocks or bonds in which the fund invests. You can, however, often move from fund to fund within a large family of funds run by a single investing group without additional transaction charges. A considerable *caution* here, though: While money market mutual funds usually carry small management fees and seldom charge any sales fees at all, many stock and bond funds charge very heavy front-loaded, back-loaded, and otherwise-loaded sales fees. The front-loaded fees, often running as high as 8–9 percent, are particularly damaging, as they lose you a substantial chunk of your money before you even begin to have it invested for you by the management of the mutual fund.

Insurance companies also offer IRAs. Here you may invest either in an IRA that is very much like a mutual fund (and with the same sales charge hazards), or in an annuity contract, with fixed monthly payouts after a specified time or at a specified age. More on the investments as investments later in this book, but a substantial *caution* here: Insurance company sales and administration fees have historically been very high, as compared with bank and no-load mutual fund fees. These too are passive IRAs and are much harder to move out of than most other IRAs, because of the nature of the insurance policies involved.

Some *companies* also have set up IRA plans for their employees, as part of the company benefits package, with the companies handling administration and its costs, doing payroll deductions if desired, and developing the plan through a sponsoring bank, insurance company, or mutual fund.

There is no particular virtue in handling your IRA through your company, but there are some disadvantages. The only savings you are likely to make are modest yearly fees; as we have seen, bank and no-load mutual fund plans you can set up on your own can cost very little. You have no control over the company's choice of IRA custodians or investment choices, as you have when you control your own plan. You cannot wait until April 15 to make last year's contributions to your IRA plan. And you cannot set up a plan that includes you and a nonworking spouse. Taking all that into account, it seems far better to set up and control your own plan, exercising that control by choosing kinds of investments, choosing custodians, shifting your IRA money as and when you see fit, and (if desired) even handling the individual trades in your own IRA investment portfolio.

Brokerage firms and recently *stock trading organizations attached to banks* offer the "self-directed" IRA account. This is essentially a straightforward brokerage account, in which you make each stock and bond trading decision yourself, with or without the advice of a stockbroker. Through it, you can invest in a wide range of investments, limited only by certain legal restrictions on what kinds of investments you can use an IRA for and on borrowing money through an IRA.

A *caution* here: Although they give you maximum control of your IRA money, self-directed IRA brokerage accounts cost a good deal to maintain. In many instances, you will have to pay as much as $50 to open the account and as much as $50 per year to maintain it. You will also have to pay trading fees on each buy or sell of stocks or bonds, fees that can swiftly mount up over the course of a year; these, plus the opening and maintenance fees, substantially cut the amount of money you can make with your money in this kind of account. In addition, it is possible to find yourself dealing with a broker who stimulates your buying and selling activity unnecessarily, to generate brokerage commissions. In both the stock brokerage and insurance industries this is called churning. It is unethical, and also illegal, but it happens, sometimes in such a borderline way as to be virtually unprovable. Beware the broker who constantly recommends small in-and-out trades, even if you make some money on those trades. It may be all right and only honest activity aimed at making you some money; but be careful, whether you are dealing with an IRA or a normal brokerage account.

There is a hidden extra cost for small investors in the self-directed account, as well. Small nunbers of shares, called odd lots, cost more to trade per share than do normal trades in multiples of one hundred shares. In terms of fees and commissions, then, the deck is very much stacked against the small investor. If you do decide to use a self-directed IRA, by all means lean toward using a discount broker or a bank-connected brokerage operation offering discount rates. You will probably save about half of what you would otherwise have to pay in brokerage fees and commissions by doing so, and that can be a big saving.

On the other hand, trading through an IRA has some real advantages. You don't have to worry about short-term capital gains or long-term capital gains; you don't have to worry about capital gains at all while you are trading. All your gains are very long-term capital gains, accumulating tax-free and taxed at ordinary income rates when distributed perhaps decades later. Note, however, that some investments are appropriate for IRAs, and some are not, as we will now discuss.

SOME THINGS YOU CAN'T DO WITH AN IRA ACCOUNT

Some kinds of investments are, by law, prohibited to IRAs. You can't put IRA money into gold, silver, gemstones, or collectibles. You can put it into gold or silver mining shares, but not directly into the metals themselves. Before 1982 you were allowed to have collectibles in your IRA account; and if you have any in your IRA account from before that year, you can continue to hold onto them, storing them with the custodian of the account. If you sell any collectibles held in your IRA account, however, you must use the money to buy legal IRA investments, not more prohibited investments.

You can't borrow money when investing your IRA money. That rules out a large body of leveraged arrangements and kinds of investments, in which one of the main objects of the investment is to make money on borrowed money. Therefore, you can't participate as a limited or general partner in a real estate venture in which mortgage money has to be borrowed, although you can invest in certain nonborrowing limited partnerships. *Caution*: With all such real estate ventures for small investors, with IRA money or taxable money, be very careful to know a good deal about the real estate investment as a business investment before you put money into it. Many such ventures are essentially tax shelters, possibly good for people with large incomes, but not necessarily for small investors. And many have been heavily skimmed—that is, milked by their promoters—before the investor even puts money into them.

Because you cannot borrow in conjunction with IRA investments, your self-directed brokerage account, by law, cannot be a margin account, in which the broker lends you part of the money to buy securities. Nor can you invest in commodities futures or other futures, which require buying at a small fraction of the actual cost of the goods being speculated in, for the nature of the transaction requires the prohibited use of borrowed money. Similarly, you may not sell borrowed stock—that is, sell "short"—with IRA money. In sum, the law prohibits the use of IRA money in a good many highly speculative investments, as the intent of Congress was to provide a means by which small savers and investors would be encouraged to grow their retirement funds as safely as is reasonably possible.

You cannot use IRA money to buy life insurance, though you can use it to buy annuities, which pay off either to you at the end of the policy term or to your named beneficiaries in the event of your untimely death. For IRA purposes, these annuities are seen as mainly investments, rather than life insurance vehicles.

SOME THINGS YOU SHOULDN'T DO WITH AN IRA ACCOUNT

Two kinds of investments make very little sense for IRA money: tax-sheltered investments and legal but still speculative investments.

Municipal bonds and other tax-sheltered investments make little sense for IRAs. Their main appeal is their tax shelter, but IRAs are themselves tax-sheltered, and no

additional tax avoidance results from such IRA investments. If you are using a municipal bond purchase to
avoid taxes on bond income—and the income is high
enough and the bond safe enough—the purchase may
make investment sense. But to put IRA money into a
municipal bond that pays some percentage points less
than comparable investments, while probably being less
safe than comparable investments, makes no sense at all.

Speculations are a different matter. My view of what
constitutes a speculation may be very different from yours.
The country is certainly full of IRA account owners running self-directed brokerage accounts that go heavily and
quickly in and out of small, fast-moving company stocks.
It is also equally full of IRA account owners who have
invested in aggressive growth mutual funds.

Some speculations are quite obviously to be avoided.
Many brokerage firms won't even let their IRA accounts
speculate in stock options, called by brokers puts and
calls. Some will discourage the purchase of new stock
issues, always a speculative practice, though others will
allow it.

It is very unwise to invest your retirement money in
speculative stocks, including both those you may buy in
a self-directed account and those you may buy through
aggressive growth mutual funds managed by investment
professionals. If we have learned anything at all about
stock market behavior from the experiences of 1929 and
the late 1960s, it is that *what goes up quickly in the stock
market must inevitably come down at least as quickly,
always at a strikingly inconvenient and often at a fatally
damaging time.* It is saddening to see reputable newspapers and magazines once again running articles about
small investors who are making "fortunes" by speculating
in fast-moving and highly questionable stocks; and it is

pathetic to see such "winners" in the process of developing the kinds of bad investing habits that can and may ruin them for their lifetimes.

Almost equally so, it is saddening to see small investors once more putting their money—and especially their retirement money—into aggressive growth mutual funds composed largely of the same kinds of highly questionable stocks. There is no way to get the kind of growth widely advertised and touted by many of these funds except by speculation, even in a rising market. We saw the same thing in the late 1960s; there were funds and superfunds and even "funds of funds." They all went down when the market went down, as they must. *The most aggressive—that is, the most speculative of them—went down the farthest, sometimes accompanied by great scandals.*

Don't speculate with your retirement money. Aside from the speculations you can't make, try to avoid all the other speculations you can legally get yourself into. Avoid such speculations as puts, calls, new issues, highly volatile gold and silver stocks, and mutual funds organized to engage in futures speculations. Also avoid highly volatile common stocks, whether you buy them yourself in a self-directed way, or through professionals speculating in them for you through aggressive growth mutual funds. For IRA money, speculative investments are not only imprudent but often fatal for your financial health.

SOME THINGS YOU SHOULD DO WITH AN IRA ACCOUNT

If you don't yet have an IRA and have any earnings at all, do set one up. If you already have one, by all means build it, putting as much as you can into it each year up to the maximum legally allowed. Don't worry too much about having to take money out of it at penalty rates later in life; as we have seen, you are likely to come out way ahead even if you must tap it later for real needs.

Treasure the forced savings aspect of an IRA. Aside from true emergency needs, it is so obviously harmful to take money out of an IRA too soon that you are unlikely to touch your IRA funds until you are at least fifty-nine and one half. That's wonderful; in a world full of all kinds of reasons to spend and all kinds of reasons to fear the future, to have your own personal retirement fund accumulating tax-free can be a great relief.

Be aware also that, as the law now stands, IRA money can't be touched by others if you are forced to declare personal bankruptcy. It just sits there, accumulating, safe from creditors, unless you yourself choose to reach for it. That may not be true for those kinds of creditors who can normally reach through the shield of bankruptcy, such as the Internal Revenue Service, but it does mean that if you are at some future time forced to declare personal bankruptcy, you may still have funds worth hundreds of thousands of dollars growing in an IRA account. That can become an extraordinarily important matter for you in some of the most difficult times of your life.

In this period, it seems wisest to put your IRA money into bank one-year-or-less certificates of deposit (CDs) and conservatively invested no-load mutual funds stressing income growth. (No load means no sales charges when buying or selling the mutual fund, and only small management fees, such as one half of one percent of portfolio value.) The bank certificates of deposit should carry no fees or commissions of any kind. When you buy either CDs or mutual funds, be very sure that all charges are specified and in writing. If the continuing charges increase while you are holding them, look for other CD's and mutual funds, assuming that the facts of competition will ensure that you will be able to find some.

While you should avoid speculative investments, being careful with your retirement money doesn't mean avoiding common stocks for the rest of your life. Far from it. There can come a time when direct purchase or purchase through mutual funds of high quality corporate stocks can be excellent retirement fund investment strategy. If there is a long, strong economic upturn at some time in the future, it may pay to move some of your IRA money into mutual funds stressing investments in the growth of blue-chip corporate stocks. If you have $40,000 or more in your IRA accounts in such a period, it may pay to take $20,000 of it and develop a self-directed account with a discount broker and yourself invest your IRA money in such blue-chip stocks. Then you will be able to buy in lots of one hundred shares (called round lots) as well as to back your own conservative good judgment in market matters. Let me stress here that I in no way regard the modest economic upturn of the early 1980s as a time for such retirement money investments. An economy moving sluggishly up and down around a stagnant center can generate considerable stock market activity, but the market in those circumstances can fluctuate swiftly and nervously. That kind of market is for speculators and some kinds of investment professionals; it is not for small investors working with their IRA money.

Watch that IRA money. Watch the banks it is in, not taking the good health of even the largest banks in the world for granted. In a world with over $600 billion in questionable international debts out there, no American bank is entirely safe. Watch the mutual funds, no

matter how conservatively invested, with shaky American
and world economies. Watch the total economic situation, for there may come a time when you will choose
to pay the early withdrawal penalties and get some of
your money out of all such investments and into harder
goods—or when the penalties you may have to pay for
withdrawal are less than they used to be.

Watch the law governing IRAs, too. There will be
changes, especially regarding larger contribution limits
and different tax arrangements as the years go by. We
are seeing the growth of huge tax-free funds here; in
future, governments may try to tax those funds and their
payouts, by higher tax rates on transactions and higher
income tax rates on later-life payouts.

REAL YIELD FROM YOUR IRA

Watch also the real yield from your total IRA investment
each year, after deducting all fees and commissions; when
comparing kinds of investments, it is the real net that
matters, after all costs are subtracted and all the various
compoundings have been done. Don't under any circumstances glumly accept fees and charges as "the cost
of doing business." Look for the least expensive—while
still entirely effective—ways of doing your money business. Bear in mind that if you put $1,000 into an in-
vestment yielding 10 percent, but wind up after all fees
and commissions at the end of the year with $990, all
that has happened is that you have lost $10 and made
nothing, no matter how nice the figures look and how
fancy the computer forms on which they are printed.

The real yield from your IRA money has to be seen
in another way, as well. Only by comparing real annual

yield with the rate of inflation can you get a serious look at what your long-run yield really is. We are all seeing a lot of financial industry ads and hearing a lot of selling talk about how you are going to make a million dollars with your $2,000 a year IRA account. Sure you will— but it is quite obvious that your million dollars, many years later, will be worth only a small fraction of what a million dollars is worth today. How small a fraction that will be depends upon the rate of inflation between then and now, and how that will work out is largely a matter of informed guesswork.

My own guess is that we are not likely to enter upon another huge, sustained bout with runaway inflation for some years, probably at least through the 1980s and beyond. Nor do I believe we are likely to encounter the kind of worldwide economic collapse that would call all financial arrangements into question and cause you to hoard gold, guns, and canned goods, while waiting for a whole new economic system to emerge. Barring either catastrophe, we are likely to see relatively safe interest rates, considerably higher than the current rate of inflation, for some years to come. Under those circumstances, the difference between what you can accumulate tax-free in an IRA and what you can accumulate in post-tax dollars can be at least the difference between pushing considerably ahead or falling somewhat behind the rate of inflation. For example, if you are paying total taxes in your highest tax bracket of 30 percent, have 10 percent interest rates available, and have an IRA, you may be gaining 3 percent a year on inflation in a year with a 7 percent inflation rate. Without an IRA, at a post-tax 7 percent, you would only be holding your own as against the rate of inflation. If you can get 11 pecent—just 1 percent more net—you can pick up 4 percent a year against the rate of inflation. But if you pay too little attention to fees and commissions, you may pick up 1 percent less and do only 2 percent better than the rate of inflation. If you speculate, you may pick up much more—but you may also lose your shirt. This is a game that goes to the tortoise, not the hare.

Two percent, 3 percent, 4 percent—none of that sounds much like a million dollars. Well, it's not, but it can be a substantial stake in real dollars a quarter century or more from now, for the differences between those percentages loom larger and larger as the years and decades go by. If you put $2,000 a year into an IRA starting at age thirty, and start pulling money out of it at age seventy, forty years later, after it grows all those years at an apparent 11–12 percent each year, you will have $1.5 million or so showing the year you start pulling your money out. If you adjust for inflation and have a real IRA money growth rate of 4 percent in those years, that is "only" the equivalent of a little under $200,000 in today's terms. However, a nest egg of $200,000 in real dollars can become the difference between good later years and very bad later years, between a reasonably good standard of living and abject poverty. Looked at that way, the IRA buildup becomes so desirable as to be indispensable, even though the inflated selling claims of the moment are clearly nonsense.

KEOGH PLANS

Many small savers and investors can set up Keogh plan retirement accounts, so-named after the congressman who sponsored the legislation making such plans possible. If you are self-employed, part time or full time, or are a sole proprietor or partner in an unincorporated business, or are employed in a business that has a Keogh plan and meet eligibility requirements, you can have a Keogh plan. Indeed, if you are employed by a business that has a Keogh plan, you will get your plan contribution free, as a fringe benefit, because sole proprietors and partners setting up such plans for themselves are forced, by law, to provide and pay for such plans for employees who work over 1,000 hours a year in the business and have been working in the business for three years or more.

If you are eligible, you can set up a Keogh plan, even though you also have an IRA. The employee of an unincorporated business, or a corporate employee who has a part-time business or free-lance occupation on the side, for example, may have both an IRA and a Keogh plan at the same time.

Keogh plans are particularly good for such high income self-employed people as doctors, lawyers, dentists, and other such professionals, and for the owners of substantial money-making businesses with very few or no employees. You can make far larger legal contributions to Keogh plans than to IRAs—if you have the income—and build up very large retirement funds as a result. At this writing, you can put as much as 20 percent of your net income—that is, all business income minus all business expenditures—up to a ceiling of $30,000 every year into a tax-free Keogh account. The money you put in is fully deductible from your taxes that year and builds up tax-free until you begin to take it out.

Some high-income people take advantage of a second kind of Keogh plan, the defined benefit plan, in which allowable maximum yearly tax-free contributions depend on how much you want to take out in the payout years, rather than on current income. In this kind of plan, you can specify a yearly payout, up to a legal limit (currently in the $100,000 yearly range), and with the help of a complex set of calculations done by your accountants and pension planners come up with legal tax-free yearly limits much higher than the $30,000 limit in the first kind of Keogh plan.

Unfortunately, not many small savers and investors will need to worry about whether they can put $30,000 or $100,000 into a Keogh plan in any given year. But many can find a Keogh plan very useful, for there may be years in which IRA contribution limits are smaller than the amounts you may be able to put into your retirement funds. You need not put money into your Keogh plan every year, any more than you need to do so with an IRA. Here, too, you can put in as much money as you want up to legal limits, put it in whenever you want, and skip some years altogether, as desired.

In most respects, Keogh plans operate much as do IRAs. Many of the same financial organizations offering IRAs also offer Keoghs and on much the same terms, except that Keoghs often cost a little more to administer because of additional paperwork; you therefore will often have to pay higher yearly administrative fees than with IRAs. You can also become trustee of your own Keogh plan, which cannot be done with an IRA, but the paperwork involved makes that an undesirable course of action for small savers and investors.

One significant difference between IRAs and Keoghs is that you can put up to 50 percent of your Keogh money each year into the purchase of life insurance that pays death benefits, which you cannot do with IRA money.

Another significant difference is that, at present, lump-sum distributions of Keogh money after age fifty-nine and one half get favorable income tax treatment, in the form of ten-year income averaging, as compared with the current five-year averaging allowed on IRA lump-sum distributions, according to ordinary income taxing rules. For those retiring soon with Keogh plans, that is a very significant tax advantage. For those retiring later, it can be significant—but the farther off your retirement, the greater likelihood of tax changes that will affect tax advantages and disadvantages.

Premature withdrawals from Keoghs suffer the same kinds of 10 percent penalties as apply to such IRA withdrawals. But you also are then not allowed to make any more contributions to your Keogh plan for the next five years; so, in fact, premature withdrawals from Keoghs carry significantly heavier penalties than from IRAs.

Tens of millions of small savers and investors have set up IRAs in the past several years. Millions more, able to save more long-term money than the maximums allowed in IRAs, have opened Keogh accounts, as well. Together, IRAs and Keoghs continue to be the best investments in the world for small savers and investors.

CHAPTER 4

Investing in Stocks: The Basics

Not so long ago, when someone asked you, "How did the market do today?" you could very easily answer, "It went up [or down] five points," and be very easily understood. Questioner and answerer were both referring to the Dow Jones industrial average, composed of thirty well-known common stocks, the most-watched financial average in the world. Then, as now, there were as many markets as there were kinds of investments, but most investors, and certainly the overwhelming majority of small investors, never got into them. Small investors traded stocks and bonds in "the" market. They didn't get into such then-esoteric matters as commodities futures, stock options, financial futures, municipal bonds, and tax shelters. You couldn't trade gold because it was against the law. Futures and options were for professionals and speculators, and some kinds of futures trading were either prohibited by law or not yet organized into trading markets. Municipal bonds and tax shelters were for the rich. Real estate was a matter of taking a few second mortgages or buying some local investment property.

For better or worse, this has all now very greatly changed. In the era of the financial supermarket, the "customer's man [or woman]" has become today's all-purpose financial services representative, and no longer handles only trades in stocks and bonds, but also sells many other kinds of investments, as do today's banker, insurance salesperson, and mutual funds seller. Quite properly, under the circumstances, there is even a brand new kind of investment professional, the Certified Financial Adviser (CFA), who attempts to bring it all together and develop individual lifetime financial plans for often-bewildered investors. And it *can* be bewildering. All the investments and all the eager sellers out there can lead some people to make very adventurous and foolish investment decisions, can prompt others to adopt unnecessarily cautious conservatism (certainly better than adventuring, but also costly in the long run), and can cause others to throw up their hands in despair and entrust their money to professionals of varying quality.

Small investors have a particularly difficult problem here. People with substantial sums to invest can afford to hire financial advisers and accountants, and those who sell investments will try to meet their needs because of the commissions their investments generate. But small investors cannot afford to hire expensive professional help, nor can they expect to get sustained high-quality attention from investment sellers. Therefore, small investors are largely dependent on their own information gathering and thinking, much more than are people with a good deal of money to invest.

All that places a lifelong premium on doing two kinds of things. First, you must teach yourself the basics of investment, such as the language, the mechanics, how to track the progress of your own and other possible investments, how to cut the cost of service charges, what to look for in a potential investment, and what main traps are to be avoided. Second, you must keep up with the world of investment.

The first need is served by books like this one and by one or more courses on the basics of investment. Such courses are now given all over the country and are usually quite inexpensive, as they are to be found as adult education courses at a local high school or service organization or at a local college. Books are good for this purpose, but if you start out unfamiliar with the language, mechanics, and trends in the world of investment, books together with courses are a much better idea. A good course will provide the basis for a lifelong and ever-increasing familiarity with the world of investment and can pay you dividends a thousand times over during your lifetime.

Books and courses will also help you to understand what you read in such publications as the *Wall Street Journal, The New York Times,* or the nearest big city newspaper that has a substantial financial section. You should subscribe to at least one of these. They will also help you to read the information available in many public libraries today, in the form of large loose-leaf investment encyclopedias, such as Moody's and Standard and Poor's. Librarians will be delighted to direct you to the sources of financial information in their libraries; that is what they are there for. But you must be able to read and understand what you are looking at, and for most small investors that will take considerable application. It's well worth the time and attention, though. Good investment decisions are not a matter of "listening to the right people," but rather a matter of exercising your own good and informed judgment.

COMPARING SHARES AND
OTHER INVESTMENTS

When you buy a share of stock, you literally buy a piece of the ownership of a company. If a company has issued altogether a million shares of stock, you own one millionth of the company, sharing the risks and rewards of that ownership with all other shareholders. The company and its management owes you nothing but its best efforts to make the company successful; a share of stock is not any kind of debt obligation. You may or may not get dividends, and the value of your share may or may not grow as it is traded during your period of ownership. There are two ways to look at what your share of that company is worth—the short-term and the long-term.

To the in-and-out-quick stock trader, the share is worth whatever its price is today on the stock market, minus whatever taxes you are likely to have to pay on any gain when you sell it. As we have seen, the tax question does not apply to IRAs and Keoghs, but does apply to other trades.

Gains on stocks held for less than six months are *short-term* gains. For tax purposes, these are treated as ordinary income for the year in which they are sold. You can subtract short-term losses that year from short-term gains, but when considering a trade on which you will make money during the course of the year, it is wise to think of the gain as all gain. (The exception, of course, is when your losses by then are so large that you can be sure that any gains you now make will be more than offset by previous losses.) Therefore, for example, if you buy a stock for $40 per share and sell it for $43, five months later, and if you are paying taxes that year in a top 33 percent bracket for all income taxes combined, what you really will be making on the sale is not $3 per share, but $2 per share ($3 less one third for taxes). This is 5 percent of the $40 you spent, minus transaction charges. On the other hand, you have held it only for five months, which means that you have to multiply $2 by 2.4 to get an "annualized" figure of $4.80, or 12 percent, to compare the money you have made to the money you might have made had you invested in something else. That is a rough example, for the tax aspects are much more complicated than this, but it is the essence of the figuring you have to do to make proper comparisons on short-term gains.

If you hold the share for six months and then sell, your gain (if any) is a *long-term capital gain*, which is offset against similar losses. The tax is less on that, amounting to 40 percent of what you might have had to pay on a short-term gain. For example, your tax on such gains, if you are in that combined 33 percent bracket, becomes 40 percent of 33 percent, or a little over 13 percent. Then your anticipated gain per share becomes $2.61, rather than $2, and your annualized gain becomes 13.05 percent.

The other way to look at what your share is worth is the view of the long-term holder: The share is worth what it yields overall, combining growth in market value and after-tax dividends (before-tax dividends for IRA and Keogh holdings). For example, a share worth $25 in the market at the beginning of a year and $27 at the end of that year has gained two points, or two twenty-fifths, or 8 percent. If the same share had dividends of $3 per share, on which you paid taxes of 33 percent in your highest income tax bracket, you would be paying $1 in taxes and keeping $2 in dividends per share. You would then have had a yield

of $2 in growth of market value plus $2 in after-tax
dividends, for a total of $4 per share on an original market
value of $25, or an overall yield of four twenty-fifths, or
16 percent.

That 16 percent net after-tax yield is pretty good,
considering that you might earn only 9–11 percent on
your money in federally insured savings accounts, or
13–14 percent in high-grade corporate bonds. The $3
dividend is fairly realistic in today's stock markets, as it
is based on figuring corporate profits of about $6 per
share, and distribution of about half of that to stockholders, a quite reliable average rule-of-thumb figure. It
also assumes a ratio of stock price to corporate profits
(also called earnings) that year of a little over 4:1, which
is also fairly realistic in today's markets. That ratio is
called the *price-earnings ratio* and is looked at carefully
by most investment professionals when sizing up a stock
for trading purposes. For "high-flyer" companies thought
to be growing fast, perhaps in glamorous, fast-growing
fields, that ratio might be 10:1, or even higher. For companies in difficult industries—or just doing badly—that
ratio might go down as low as 2:1, or in rare instances
even lower.

But let us not leave the example too soon, for what
goes up also can go down. The same stock might not
gain 2 points in the year, but might go down to 23 from
25, losing 2 points. And the board of directors, in a bad
year, might cut dividends from $3 to $2.25 per share, so
that your after-tax dividend income is $1.50 per share.
Then a loss of $2 per share in market value plus an after-
tax $1.50 dividend yield adds up to an overall yield of
minus 50 cents per share, or minus 2 percent for the
year. That's not very good at all, because it must be
compared with what you could have earned on your
money in that federally insured savings account—which

continues to set the standard against which all other investments must be measured. If that year you could have earned 11 percent in such an account, then your stock investment cost you the 2 percent you lost plus the 11 percent you didn't gain, for a total loss of 13 percent. That's a lot, because with that 13 percent you are entirely losing the enormous values generated by the compounding of interest, of growth on top of growth.

Looking at this question of stock market investment from a somewhat wider perspective, the Dow Jones industrial average moved in the 900–1000 range during the late 1960s. By the early 1980s, it was moving in the 1100–1200 range, and its forward movement of some 200 or so points in the early 1980s was being hailed by many stock traders as a move to historic new highs. But the historic new highs were altogether a move of some 20 percent up in about fifteen years, plus whatever dividends were distributed in very difficult, low-profit times.

You might have taken the same dollar fifteen years earlier and put it into an unglamorous, federally insured bank time deposit, later called a certificate of deposit. Then you could have had 10 percent before taxes and a real 7 percent on your money during those years. If so, your dollar would almost have doubled in fifteen years, growing to $1.97—an increase of 97 percent, not 20 percent, and all federally insured and certain. Discussing this in averages obscures the huge losses suffered by many small investors in the late 1960s and early 1970s, when the stock market collapsed. Large institutions and wealthy individuals can take losses, move their money about, and do as well or better than the averages; small investors cannot, and far too often lose their shirts when stock prices fall sharply. So be careful in the stock market. No matter how good it looks at any given moment, and no matter how many wonderful success stories you see in the press and hear in the stockbroker's office, there is always substantial risk in the market.

OPPORTUNITIES IN STOCKS

With those risks, there is also always opportunity. When the stock of a large, stable American company in a reasonably healthy industry is selling at three or four times its earnings, or when the total value of its shares is less than the total value of its assets (called its *book value*), you may be looking at a stock that needs very little encouragement to go up substantially. On the other hand, its assets may be considerably overvalued; for example, a steel plant that is open and working may be worth twenty times what it is worth once closed. Then working assets become little more than scrap metals. Successful investing in the stock market requires study, watching the record of earnings and dividends, watching the behavior of the stock in the market, drawing some long-term conclusions, and buying when you think you know what you are doing, rather than because other people are buying and the price of the stock is therefore going up.

That, by the way, is called the *fundamentalist* approach to trading, and is one of the two main ways to approach the matter. The fundamentalist looks at the basics and mostly considers the individual company and its business prospects. The *chartist*, on the other hand, looks mostly at the averages for whole markets and groups of stocks, while of course considering the specifics when making buying decisions within groups of stocks. That approach is best suited to people who have enough resources to buy many different stocks and thereby spread their risks, an approach called *diversifying*. But small investors buying and selling stocks on their own haven't such resources, and must inevitably be much more fundamentalist than chartist in their approach.

When you are considering companies for stock purchase, you should first determine that they are companies with stock that is widely traded. You can determine that by seeing if the stock is traded on the New York or American Stock Exchanges, which are listed in newspapers with substantial financial sections. Some companies you may want to consider may not be traded on either exchange, but rather may be traded *over the counter*—that is, among a national network of traders, whose markets are also listed in the newspaper. In either case, you should learn more about the company and its stock by reading up on it in a standard stock reporting service at the local library.

The reason for wanting stocks you invest in to be widely traded—and, preferably, listed on these main exchanges—is that the more widely traded a stock is the less likely that it will move up and down erratically because of a few major buy or sell orders, or because a relatively small number of people are speculating in it and thereby pushing the price up—only to come crashing down. There are always small companies with a relatively small amount of stock outstanding—that is, available for trading; these are *thinly held* companies, whose stocks are often on their way up or down for no very good reason beyond fad and speculation. Small investors usually come into such stocks last, when they are at their highs, and get out too late, after they have lost their appeal and gone down fast. But this is unlikely to happen to a General Motors, IBM, or Xerox, which have so much stock outstanding that they are far more stable stock investment opportunities. On the whole, it is best for small investors on their own in the stock market to stay with large, well-known companies, especially those listed on the New York Stock Exchange. These are often called blue-chip stocks, though that description is only a general one, there never having been a list of such stocks that everyone could agree on.

There can, however, be special reasons for investing in a company, whether or not it is a blue chip. One very good reason for doing so is that you may have very special knowledge about that company, possibly because you work there. Another may be that you may have the ability to secure stock in your company at quite favorable prices through stock option plans. In neither case can you trade in-and-out-quick to take advantage of current special knowledge, as of a big new contract about to be signed or a technical breakthrough; that kind of insider dealing is prohibited by law. But you can and should seriously consider exercising stock options if you think your company is going to move ahead well; you may even buy stock in your company without stock options, if you think it will be a good investment. Someone working for Xerox or IBM way back when, before they were big companies, might have made a fortune by buying a little stock in the company or exercising some stock options; in fact, some people did make millions that way. Others made fortunes from outside, because they believed in the futures of the then-new technologies involved and the managements of those companies. These were not well-known companies then; far from it. They were little companies with big ideas, trying their best to exploit new technology. It was something of a gamble for small investors, though; such small companies always are, as each new field has many small new companies, and only a few survive. We have been seeing that most recently in the field of small computers, with many companies doing well in their early days and a subsequent inevitable shakeout.

Be careful about exercising those stock options, though, especially if you are working for a smallish, thinly traded company. You will probably have to hold optioned stock for some time before you can sell it, for tax reasons, and a thinly held stock can fluctuate a good deal. It is very painful to buy optioned stock and then watch it go down, without being able to do a thing about it.

It is even more painful if you have borrowed money to exercise your stock option. Many people have done that, only to find that high interest rates have eaten up their gains on the stock; and if the stock goes down, the combination of high interest rates and stock losses can be devastating.

TYPES OF SHARES

In form, there are two basic kinds of shares, *preferred stock* and *common stock*. Holders of preferred stock get stated amounts of dividends per share before any dividends can be issued to common stockholders and in some instances also have those dividends cumulate from year to year until paid out before common stockholders can receive dividends. Preferred stock also sometimes carries greater weight in corporate decision making than does common stock and so is very often a control device used by major shareholders and management.

Common stock is much more often the main kind of stock issued and traded by most corporations. It is stock that fully shares the risks and rewards of ownership, having no preference as to dividends but being in no way limited as to the amounts of dividends that will be paid per share. When you trade stock, you will—in almost all instances—be trading common stock.

TRADING STOCKS

The only time you are likely to trade stock directly through a company is when you buy stock directly from or sell your stock directly to a company that employs you. Otherwise, you will be moving the stock through someone performing the broker's function, either a stockbroker or a bank with a brokerage department. Up until a few years ago, you would have been trading solely through a broker, operating on a fixed industrywide fee basis, but brokerage commissions are no longer preset. As a direct result, brokerage fees have come down a great deal; discount brokers and the bank discount brokerage departments developed, pressuring the older brokerage houses to reduce their fees. In the long run, that will probably tend to equalize all brokerage fees at low levels, but right now there are wide variations. At this time, a trade of a hundred shares at $50 per share at the high commissions charged by most major stockbrokers will cost about $90. The same trade of a hundred shares at $50, handled by a discount broker or bank, will cost $35–$50, roughly half of what you might otherwise have to pay. On larger numbers of shares per trade, the savings are even more, going down to about 30–40 percent of the higher brokerage costs. Even for small investors, that can mean very substantial savings during any given year. Assuming that you make ten hundred-share trades a year in the $30–$60 per share range, perhaps five buys and five sells, your savings can come to about $500 per year, and that sum alone can make the difference between making an adequate return on your modest stockholdings and not. About the only thing a small investor will lose by moving from a high-priced broker to a discount broker is any newsletter and any specific recommendations the high-priced broker sends to its customers. Well, for $500 a year you can buy a weekly financial newspaper, like Dow Jones and Company's *Barron's,* and have money left over. You can even throw in one or more of the high-priced investment letters advertised in the *Wall Street Journal* or *Barron's,* spending a couple of hundred dollars a year for all kinds of specific investment advice and have hundreds left over from your savings. You will find quite complete listings of the major financial services available, with descriptions, addresses, and prices, in Brownstone and Carruth's *Where to Find Business Information,* which is available in most fairly substantial public libraries. Use discount brokers.

You can buy stocks for cash or you can buy them with part cash and part credit. When you buy for cash, your broker makes the trade, and you are obliged to settle up in full within five business days of the trade. When you buy partly on credit, you are buying *on margin,* which means that the broker is extending you credit for part of the purchase price of the stock, within legal limits. If you have a 50 percent margin account with your broker, you must come up with 50 percent of the cash within five business days, and on the 50 percent margin loan will pay whatever is the going rate of interest—usually a little above the prime rate—for broker's loans to customers at the time.

Small investors should be very uneasy about margin accounts. They are wonderful for *leverage*—that is, for making money with borrowed money when your stocks are going up. But when they are going down, leverage may get you into serious trouble. Assume, for example, that you have set up a 50 percent margin account with your broker and have bought two hundred shares at $50 per share, thereby putting in $5,000 in cash and owing your broker $5,000. The $10,000 worth of shares is collateral for the $5,000 brokers' loan. Then assume that the stock you bought goes down, perhaps to $35 per share. Then you still owe your broker $5,000, but your own stake is worth only $2,000, so your broker is going to have to ask you for more cash—that is *issue a margin call*. The broker has no choice; the law requires that when your *equity*—that is, the value of your stake in the shares—drops below a certain point (which varies with then-current regulations), you must either come up with enough cash to bring your account up to legal requirements or the broker must sell out enough of your stock to bring loan and equity back into legal balance. What that means, in practice, is that you will be forced either to sell out in a fast-declining market at a huge loss or to come up with more cash to hold stock that is fast losing much of its value, hoping that by holding on you can wait until it regains its value—if it will. Novels and movies have made the subsequent panic familiar to all of us. For small investors, especially, the same thing can happen today. Beware margin accounts.

Whether you buy for cash or on margin, the technical side is easy. You can tell your broker to buy or sell at the current price as of the time the trade is made, or you can specify a top price for buying and a bottom price for selling. You can tell your broker that your order is good for a specific time, such as that day, or good until you withdraw it.

You can buy stocks (and other securities) with borrowed money—that is, on margin—and hold them in the expectation that they will go up and you will sell them at a profit high enough to make you money after paying off your brokers' loans. That is called having a *long* position. You can also sell stocks (and other securities) you don't own, borrowing the stocks through your broker, on the theory that the stocks will go down between then and the time you actually have to buy them to cover your sale, and that you will make money on the difference between the price at which you sold them and the price you eventually have to pay for them. That is called selling *short*—and it is the kind of gambling game that small investors should be no means get into. The best thing that can happen to a small investor selling short is to lose a little money the first time; the worst is to make a little money and develop a ruinous habit.

KINDS OF STOCKS

In and around the stock market you will always hear and read a lot about different kinds of stocks. This one is blue chip, that one a growth stock, and the other a "special situation." Try not to pay too much attention to all that. Much of what you are hearing and reading is selling talk. A company is a company, a stock a stock. Each must be evaluated individually, rather than as part of some kind of investment "class." To help you move through the jargon a little, here is a brief guide to some of that jargon:

• A *blue-chip* stock is one that is widely held, well-regarded as a stable investment opportunity, and probably listed on the New York Stock Exchange. It has a long, uninterrupted record of paying dividends and is—as a matter of record—unlikely to fluctuate wildly. It may also have several other characteristics and also be described as, for example, a growth stock or a cyclical stock.

• A *growth* stock is one thought by some market analysts to be capable of growing in its market value very quickly, reflecting the bright prospects of its company. That is sometimes true, with small new companies in growing new industries, plowing their profits back into their businesses and growing by leaps and bounds, with the market values of their stocks growing similarly. But many such stocks are speculative, with temporary excellent stock performances and glowing annual reports masking real problems of capitalization, competition, technology, and management.

• A *high flyer* is a stock that is surging upward in market price, sometimes for good reasons and all too often only because of the investment fad of the moment. These are often small companies and also described as growth stocks, or by the name of the current fad.

• A *high technology* stock is one issued by a company that is depending for its success largely upon its position in one of the new fields created by new technology, such as a computer or biotechnology company. There certainly are such companies, and that is a valid description—but of a company, not necessarily an investment opportunity. As investments, high technology companies are a fad. The stock of some such companies will prove excellent investments. Others will be terrible. This fad for high tech stocks is the exact counterpart of the ruinous electronics company fad of the 1960s and early 1970s, in which hundreds of thousands of small investors lost tens of millions of dollars; many small electronics companies in which they had invested (because it was popular to do so) issued stock, went up fast, and when an inevitable shakeout of small new companies happened to coincide with a general stock market downturn, came down with a crash.

• A *special situation* is usually the stock of a company in deep trouble, which is being sold at so little per share that it is touted as a steal: "bound to go up—you'll at least double your money tomorrow." Well, sometimes— but not often. And it is hardly ever worth the gamble, especially for small investors. The exception is when you have special knowledge of your own—real knowledge, that is, not tips, gossip, and rumors.

There are many other kinds of stocks as well. For example, the stock of depression-prone companies, like auto manufacturers, is often described as *cyclical*, or moving with the business cycle, while the stocks of depression-resistant corporations, like telephone companies, are described as *defensive*, because they are thought to be good stocks to buy in hard times. But these generalizations really don't hold very well. When an economy moves as ours does, up and down a little around a stagnant center, the old cyclical descriptions don't apply. Nor do they prepare you for utility stocks that come crashing down because of the failure of huge and expensive atomic power projects, even in good times. The main thing with these kinds of generalizations, is to see them as only that. Keep your eye on the prospects of *the individual companies* in which you are or may be investing, not on "the market."

CHAPTER 5

Investing in Bonds: The Basics

When you buy a share of stock, you become part owner—a very small part owner—of a company, literally sharing in the risks and rewards with other shareholders. When you buy a bond, you are lending money to a government or private organization, in return for a promise that you will get your money back after a stated time and with interest. You are then functioning as lender of your own money, without passing it through a bank, as you would if you put your money into a savings account.

In modern practice, the word *bond* is a general term used to describe a good many different kinds of debt obligations, including those specifically called bonds as well as notes and bills. It is also used to describe debt obligations issued by the federal government, by private corporations, and by a wide range of municipals, which are other-than-federal governmental bodies of all kinds (not just cities). Whatever they are called and whoever issues them, the essence of the bond transaction is that you are lending your money directly to the bond issuer. If you buy a bond previously issued to someone else, you are still lending your money directly, by taking over a loan made by the original holder of the bond.

You can hold a bond until maturity, with the interest being paid to you either periodically, often on presentation of coupons attached to the bond, or cumulating with compound interest until the end of the bond's term, a less-common form. On some types of bonds, especially municipals, which are discussed in Chapter 6, the interest you earn is free from some or all taxes. At the end of the term—that is, when the bond has reached *maturity* —you are repaid the original amount—the *face value*—that you invested. Many bonds have long terms, such as ten or twenty years, but your money is not necessarily tied up when invested in such bonds, because they are traded in standard markets. Economic conditions can affect the trading value of a bond, however, so that you may find that the bond has lost or gained significantly in value at the time you wish to sell. Because the bond value can be variable, even when the initial investment is quite secure, bonds are more appropriate for long-term investments than for situations in which you may wish to get your cash out quickly, either by selling the bond or by redeeming it—that is, cashing it in before maturity.

THE QUESTION OF SAFETY

Traditionally, bonds have been thought of by small investors as rather safe investments. In a way, there is still some truth to that, as the basic difference between a debt obligation and a share makes it probable that bondholders will get some of their money out of a failure, while shareholders may lose it all. But beyond that, the wide variety of bonds available and the underlying uncertainties of this period make it necessary to be very, very careful to distinguish between the different kinds of bonds in

which you might invest. Some are as safe as any investment other than gold, guns, and grub can be; others are
as terribly unsafe as the most speculative stocks you could
possibly secure. United States government obligations,
backed as they are by the full taxing and enforcement
power of the federal government, are safe; the bonds of
many state and local governments are not. And you can
get "wonderful" rates of interest on the bonds of many
other governments, but should not touch them unless
you are a bond-trading professional—and then only very
gingerly in this period. You may find the bond devalued
or repudiated—overnight in some cases.

In this period, the question of safety is central and
must be settled to your own satisfaction before the question of yield even comes up seriously. That is a very sober
way of saying that anyone who is dazzled by high returns—and mammoth after-tax returns—may be in grave
danger of losing his or her shirt on bad bonds.

An essential step is to check the ratings of any bond
you are thinking of buying. Moody's and Standard and
Poor's both have large bond-rating publications, which
you will find in many brokerage offices and large public
libraries. Top rated—that is, safest—bonds are rated AAA
by Standard and Poor's and Aaa by Moody's, with double
A and single A bonds also very highly rated. Standard
and Poor's then goes to BBB for the fourth rating, and
Moody's to Baa—and so on all the way down to the
bottom or most speculative of the bonds on the market.
The ratings services can't and shouldn't make up your
mind for you as to the safety of a given bond, but they
can save you from making some very serious and obvious
errors. Barring crisis and mass business and state and local
government economic failures and defaults, bonds rated
triple A and double A are likely to be reasonably safe,

and single A bonds are close behind. Down in the first rank of the B's, you are on the edge of speculation, and you had better know a good deal that is favorable about a bond's issuer before buying. Beyond that, you should doubt even your favorable information, for the general opinion of informed professionals is running against you. And if a broker strongly recommends that you buy such an obviously chancy bond, it is time to think hard about whether or not to continue on with that broker, no matter how persuasive the arguments advanced for buying the bond.

Bond safety is a little more complicated than whether or not an issuer is likely to default. Full defaults are few and far between, though they do happen. Much more likely is the kind of event that can greatly harm the value of bonds you are holding, making them ruinous to sell— even though, if you hold them until they mature, you will be paid back your lent money with all promised interest in full. A bankrupt company may go right through bankruptcy back into normal operation and pay its bond-holders in full, but during the period of bankruptcy those holders might have found it impossible to sell the bonds except at huge losses. Similarly, a city—like New York in the mid-1970s—may not be able to keep up on its debt or interest payments, although in the long run it can meet all its commitments. Yet New York City bond-holders selling during that most difficult period suffered huge investment losses. The problem in those situations is that you don't really know that the company will come out of bankruptcy or that the city in partial default will get its head above water. In such situations, you may elect to hold the bond, but you may elect to sell and take your losses so that you can salvage some of your money. These are difficult decisions and best avoided by being very careful when you are considering the original investment.

Some bonds are safer than others, up through the safest federal government bonds. And some other high-yielding investments may be safer and more lucrative than many bonds. A share of IBM is a lot safer and more profitable than a Washington State utility bond in default, no matter how attractive the tax aspects of the municipal bond seemed to be at purchase. A federally insured money market account in a bank that is in deep trouble because of bad loans at home and abroad may be perfectly safe, while a share of that bank's stock may be worthless. In today's investment world, very little can be presumed safe; each investment must be evaluated on its own, not primarily as part of a group.

THE IMPACT OF CHANGING INTEREST RATES

The general rates of interest currently in being in an economy affect bond values in another way and raise the question of short- or long-term commitments. Bond prices after original issue tend to move with rates of interest. When interest rates on bonds you are holding are lower than the interest rates being paid on newly issued bonds, the market value of your bonds will tend to go down, until their effective interest rate is about the same as current interest rates. Then they are called *deeply discounted*, meaning that they have lost much of their current resale value. On the other hand, bonds with higher interest rates than those currently being paid will go up in value, being then sold at a *premium* above their stated value.

The main trend in this regard over the past decade and more has been the decline in bond values caused by steeply rising interest rates. Bonds—including many safe federal government bonds—that were issued with, for example, 6 percent per-year yields until their maturity decades later, now may be selling at half their stated (face) values. Investors holding them have been confronted with the no-win decisions of either selling out at huge losses or holding on until either maturity or the advent of lower interest rates that would push up bond values again. Those who have held their bonds have had their promised (very low) interest payments but have had to see much larger-yield opportunities pass by, thereby losing a great deal of what they might and should have made on their bond-invested money. That is why so many people have been staying with short-term debt obligations all during this period, even though some have begun to go back to longer-term debt obligations, drawn by high yields and on the theory that interest rates are bound to go down in the long run.

Maybe long-term interest rates will go down; maybe they won't. At this writing, they look as if they are about to go up again, not down. By the time you read this page, they may have gone up, gone down again, and now be promising to fluctuate some more. For that is to be reasonably expected in this very difficult period—the kind of interest rate fluctuations that make long-term prediction in this area impossible. It still seems wisest to put your money into short-term investments. If in bonds, go short-term and medium-term, not long-term—and go even medium-term with considerable care, no matter how attractive the yield and the after-tax yield look as of now.

THE QUESTION OF COLLATERAL

Considerable attention is often paid to the matter of collateral, the theory being that a bond or any other loan secured by physical assets is generally safer and therefore more desirable than an unsecured loan. But while that may be true for a banker deciding on whether or not to grant a borrower a small loan, it does not really hold true in this period for most bonds. The problem is that if a bond issuer is in the kind of trouble that causes defaults and has to sell assets backing up bonds to pay off those bonds at maturity, the sale is likely to be at scrap-and-foreclosure prices, rather than at working-asset prices. Meanwhile, your bonds will have lost much of their value in anticipation of their holders being able to collect only a few cents on the dollar eventually, if that. The main question of safety is not *what* backs the bond but *who* backs the bond.

Having said that, it should also be said that it is best—except in the instance of the United States government—to have both a general promise to pay from a sound bond issuer and the backing of that promise with collateral.

Sometimes, you will have only the general promise to pay. Technically, the bond making that promise is a *debenture*; if someone calls it that, translate that into bond, because for all practical investing purposes that is what it is. On some such occasions, a seller will make a fuss about the bond being backed by the "full faith and credit" of its issuer. Sure; but that means no collateral—it is only a bare promise to pay, unless the collateral is also specified.

On other occasions, a seller will dwell upon the value

of the collateral backing up the bond. Be sure to determine on those occasions whether or not there is also a general promise to pay—that is, whether it is also a *general obligation* bond. You may buy the bond even if it is not, as for example if it is a desirable public authority bond backed by the value of the structures under the jurisdiction of that authority. But don't buy any bond without being clear as to whether it is backed by collateral and whether it is a general obligation of its issuer, as these are key facts affection the amount of risk involved.

YIELD, RISK, AND MARKET CONDITIONS

There is in most instances a quite straightforward relationship between what a bond will yield in interest and how risky that bond is: the higher the interest, the higher the risk. Stocks are much more a kind of guessing and gambling game, because there you are betting mostly on how much the stock of a company will grow in value, with dividends usually taking a steady course and having a relatively minor role in the investment decision. But a bond is mainly a matter of interest on money lent. Only a few professionals even try to make money trading the vast majority of bonds; for small investors it is very much a matter of interest and risk.

You can understand the situation best by putting yourself into the shoes of the bond's issuer. As issuer, you want to pay as little interest as you must to attract investors who will lend you the money you seek. If the rating services and thousands of bond-market professionals think you are a low risk, you will have to pay relatively low rates of interest. The more of a risk they think you are, the higher the interest rate you will have to pay. The range of rates depends on the current state of interest rates in the economy, of course; the federal government, through the Federal Reserve Board, has a great deal to do with setting the basic interest rates within the economy at any given time, with additional impacts from such matters as federal deficits and international money market conditions. But whatever the general state of interest rates, the relationships remain the same—the higher the risk, the higher the interest.

That is why a three-month Treasury bill pays so little; the risk is negligible and the term is short. That is also why a high-grade blue-chip corporate bond pays a few points more than such a federal obligation, while paying less than a bond issued by a second rank corporation, and being graded accordingly by the rating services and other bond professionals. That is also why municipal bonds pay so very much, once you take their tax breaks into account; they are on the whole very risky investments. If they were not, their issuers would be able to pay less interest on them.

You rarely really lock in high yields on long-term bonds when you buy them. Most bonds are *callable*, meaning that their issuers can pay them off in full early—often very early—in their lives, if interest market conditions change enough to make it worthwhile. A bond may pay 15 percent when conditions make it necessary, but if conditions change so that money can be raised on 8 percent bonds, issuers will recall their outstanding bonds and issue new bonds at the 8 percent rate.

One kind of corporate bond, the *convertible bond*, carries an additional element of possible reward. These kinds of bonds carry the privilege of converting your bondholding into a stockholding, at a preset price per share for a specified time. This can be valuable if the market value of the stock goes up beyond that preset price. You will have to pay in advance for the possible reward, though, as these kinds of bonds may pay a point or so less in interest than the same bonds without the conversion privilege.

Another kind of bond is popular as of this writing: the *zero coupon bond*, so-named because it pays no cash interest at all until maturity, and then matures with compounded interest in place, for many times the amount you paid for it. *Caution:* The zero coupon bond is not a tax-sheltered investment, like an IRA or Keogh plan. The unpaid interest that accrues and compounds in the bond every year is treated as ordinary income that year for tax purposes. Another *caution:* These bonds can fluctuate in value during their lifetime much more than most interest-paying bonds, because they do not have the normal interest payments that tend to smooth out yearly bond yields. On the whole, small investors should be wary of zero coupon bonds. To pay a few thousand dollars now for a bond that will pay you $20,000 after the turn of the century may seem attractive, but it really may be no better than any other relatively stable investment with the interest left in to compound and may yield considerably less than far more liquid investments.

CORPORATE BONDS

Corporations go into debt in three basic ways. They borrow money directly from banks and other financial institutions, issue short-term, large-denomination notes bought by such institutions, and issue medium- and long-term bonds bought by individuals and institutions. Small investors cannot afford to buy the short-term notes as individuals, except as part of mutual fund portfolios when they buy shares in mutual funds. Small investors can and do buy corporate bonds, usually for a combination of safety, relatively high yield, and stable income.

Most corporate bonds pay fixed rates of interest until maturity, though in recent years some have carried variable rates of return. As previously discussed, almost all are callable, should interest rates lower, allowing less interest to be paid on borrowings. Some are convertible, and a few are zero coupon in nature.

Medium-term fixed-interest bonds issued by blue-chip corporations can be quite good investments for small investors. They must be watched, of course, like any investment, but they tend to be relatively safe and fluctuate relatively little in value during their lifetimes, when compared with stocks and municipal bonds. They are not federally insured, as are bank money market accounts, but in one sense that is an advantage. The need to attract buyers to corporate bonds forces corporate issuers to pay higher rates of interest than federally insured bank money market accounts or federally issued bonds offer. As we have seen, an extra 2–4 percent compounding over the years can make an enormous difference at the end of a few decades, and high-grade, relatively low-risk corporate bonds can provide that kind of difference.

Do be sure to buy the bonds of very large blue-chip companies, even though you will see other well-rated bonds paying a percent or two—or three—more in interest. Even among large companies, it is wise to apply the same kind of careful thinking that you apply to stock purchases. An industry that is clearly becoming rapidly obsolete, such as the American steel industry, has large companies issuing well-rated bonds that you should not

purchase—not because the companies are currently un-
profitable, but because their long-term prospects are poor.
An industry that clearly has a mountainous problem
hanging over it, such as the problem created by the American banking industry's huge bad loans abroad, is an
industry you should not be lending money to. Depositing
money in federally insured accounts is one thing: lending
money to the banking industry through purchase of its
bonds is quite another.

Those corporate bonds that are not backed by specific
collateral are also called *debentures*; they are "full faith
and credit" general obligations—that is, bare promises
to pay. Those that are backed by collateral usually are
backed by corporate property—by first mortgages, second, or even third mortgages, though often called by
other names, or by any of several other kinds of arrangements and instruments, always going back to the value
in the property itself. If you do decide to rely on the
presence of such collateral at all in making your bond
purchase decision, look in the prospectus for a clear description of the collateral and its location, and from there
try to develop an opinion as to how well the collateral
would keep its value in the event of corporate troubles.
For example, a bond collateralized by a going plant full
of machinery rapidly becoming obsolete in a one-industry
town often might as well not be collateralized at all. If
the plant shuts down, the machinery will be salable for
junk metal, and the land the plant stands on may not be
salable at all, becoming a tax drain rather than a source
of funds with which to pay bondholders. On the other
hand, the same plant, located on land that can be con-
verted to residential or office realty uses in the heart of
a growing city, may be worth more as land than as a
going plant and be excellent bond collateral. The truth

is that there are no very good shortcuts to sound investment decisions; you have to learn enough to understand
the possible risks and rewards, and that takes time and
attention.

FEDERAL DEBT OBLIGATIONS

This is the one area in which not all debt obligations are
popularly described as bonds. That is because the federal
government is such a huge borrower that the kinds of
debt obligations have become quite well known by their
separate names. There are Treasury bills, Treasury notes,
federal bonds, special savings bonds, and an increasingly
large number of agency debt obligations, known by the
names of the issuing agencies.

The federal debt is now well over $1 trillion and is
headed very rapidly toward the $2 trillion mark. These
are meaningless figures as figures; they are really too large
to comprehend. But they are very meaningful figures in
terms of impact, for the United States government is by
far the largest single debtor in the world, mainly to its
own people; that has huge consequences for the stability
of the American and world economies. With that kind
of national debt, the hazard of runaway inflation in-
creases, and with it the possibility that all debt holders
will get their interest and principal back in dollars worth
much less than those they originally put in. But not yet;
in this period, American federal government debt obligations are the safest to be found anywhere in the world
and should be treated as such.

Let me immediately qualify that: The longer-term
regular federal obligations are traded, like any other bonds;
thus, although they are safe in terms of their *stated in-*

terest payments and *payouts of principal* at maturity, nevertheless like other traded bonds they can gain or lose value during their lifetimes due to interest rate fluctuations.

Before the deregulation of bank interest, short-term Treasury bills became prime investment instruments for small investors. During the 1970s and early 1980s, millions of small investors began to buy them, drawn by their great safety, their liquidity, and the relatively high interest rates they paid, especially when compared with the old 5¼–5¾ percent savings accounts. Some small investors bought them directly, but most bought them through banks and brokers, paid the transaction fees, and considered themselves lucky to have that kind of investment available in very uncertain times. And they were.

Now that has all changed, for with the advent of federally insured bank money market funds, small investors can get just as much safety and higher interest besides, without transaction fees and with no inconvenience. Some small investors are still buying short-term Treasury bills, but it is no longer really necessary, unless you believe that the banking system is about to collapse and that you may not be able to get at your money when you need it. Liquid money market accounts normally pay ½ percent to 1 percent over short-term Treasury bill rates. And unlike longer-term counterparts, these Treasury bills are not tradable.

Treasury notes, running one to ten years, are also available, and these pay somewhat higher rates of interest but still not more than comparable longer-term certificates of deposit (CDs). They are tradable and—like other bonds—fluctuate with money market conditions. They do pose a special problem, in that although they can sometimes be bought directly but quite inconveniently from the government, the main way of buying them is through bond brokers, who charge transaction charges that can bring down the effective rate of interest by a full 1 percent and sometimes more. As a result this kind of investment is questionable.

Longer-term Treasury bonds, negotiable and running ten years and longer, are issued in large denominations, and small investors are likely to participate in them only through mutual fund purchases, rather than directly.

Savings bonds, aimed at and sold hard to consumers in both world wars and beyond, may attract some small investors for patriotic reasons. That is purely a matter of personal choice, rather than a matter of seeking return on money. Savings bonds are nonnegotiable and are certainly safe enough, in terms of interest and principal repayment. Interest is exempt from state and local taxes, and federal taxes are deferred until you actually cash in on some kinds of savings bonds—at this writing, the EE series carries that feature. But if you redeem the bond early, there is an interest penalty. And whether you redeem early or late, these bonds have historically carried lower yields than comparable investments.

Federal agency debt obligations are quite a different matter. These are federally guaranteed and normally carry higher rates of interest than do either short-term Treasury bills or federally insured bank accounts. Some require higher minimum unit investments than most small investors can afford, but some do not, and there is constant pressure to lower minimum investments, making them more accessible to small investors. There are transaction charges here, too, but the higher interest rates available can more than make up for them. Such agencies as the Small Business Administration (SBA), the Government

National Mortgage Association (Ginny Mae, which issues bonds called Ginny Maes), and a dozen others are
all out in the financial marketplace, continually raising
money. They are well worth consideration by small investors.

Caution: With the concerted attempt to "privatize"
some aspects of government activities in the past several
years, has come the development of some private companies that may seem like government agencies. When
these raise money, they very carefully state in large clear
print that they are not government agencies, but very
often they are taken for such agencies anyway. These are
not federally guaranteed bonds and may therefore carry
unknown risks. For example, there are the "Sallie Maes,"
bonds issued to fund student loans but by a private corporation. They may be quite safe and may even be in-
directly backed by government funds, but in difficult
times there can be a world of difference between an
absolute federal guarantee and anything less.

CHAPTER 6

Municipal Bonds: Look Before You Leap

Municipal bonds have become a bigger and bigger business in the 1980s. Hundreds of thousands of large- and medium-sized investors, and some small investors, too, have bought tens of billions of dollars worth of these tax-exempt state and local debt obligations every year, drawn by the high after-tax yields offered. In this, they have been encouraged vigorously by hundreds of securities firms, who have been selling municipals hard, as is so clearly demonstrated by the multitude of ads for municipals in every major newspaper.

It has not been this way for very long. As recently as twenty-five years ago, municipals were considered suitable only for the very rich. Their yields were very small, since they were generally quite safe, and only high-tax-bracket investors were able to save enough in taxes to make them worthwhile buys. And they were indeed worthwhile, yielding after taxes as much as two or three percentage points more than comparable risks, because of the tax exemption. Then, as now, the interest on state and local debt obligations was exempt from federal income taxes. To state residents, municipals may also be exempt from state taxes, and to local residents from local taxes as well. That is the *triple tax exempt* investment so heavily promoted—a bond that, because of where you live, may be exempt from all income taxes.

In a way, the increasing popularity of municipals has been the strangest development of the post-World War II era. Municipals have become popular investments largely because they have become riskier investments, with their issuers therefore being forced to pay much higher rates of interest than in earlier periods. There is a deep and continuing crisis in American state and local government, with scores of major cities and thousands of smaller cities, towns, and local authorities of all kinds forever teetering on the edge of bankruptcy. As a direct result, the vast majority of state and local debt obligations, lumped together and called municipal bonds, *are far riskier investments than any federal government debt obligations and also considerably riskier than most blue-chip corporate debt obligations.* That is why their net after-tax yield is larger for many medium-income investors and much larger for many large-income investors—and that is the only reason. Don't lose sight of that very straightforward fact in the face of a barrage of hard selling talk.

A surprisingly large number of small savers and investors are also buying municipal bonds, even though they are least helped by the tax advantages they bring. That is a tribute to the skills of those who are selling these bonds, for their available after-tax yields to small investors are often only slightly higher than those available in much safer investments—indeed, they are actually lower than those available in some considerably safer investments.

On the other hand, some small savers and investors will find specific municipals attractive investments. For example, someone living in a smallish, fairly affluent suburban town or city may find a locally originated bond particularly attractive. In such a situation, you may know a great deal about the town or city and think highly of the safety of the issue, even though bond-rating services may not quite agree with you. You should be wary of buying any bond, locally originated or otherwise, that is rated in the Bs or less by the rating services; however you may well think that a bond rated A (which is the *third rank down*, after all—don't be misled by that A) is really worth a double or even a triple A. When that happens— *and the knowledge is really your own, not someone's sales pitch*—you may be looking at an investment with rewards considerably outweighing risks, even in a municipal bond. In your home community, you will also probably be dealing with a bond that is indeed triply tax exempt and therefore has a little extra appeal. You may even be dealing with a bond on which local authorities have tacked special incentives for local people to buy, reasoning that they can thus obtain much otherwise-hard-to-get funding right at home. In these respects, buying a local bond issue may be quite equivalent to buying the stock of your own company. When you know a lot about a possible investment before you even begin to make an investment decision, you can make a sound decision far more easily than when you must rely on secondhand information, and much less of it.

Note here that this recommendation does not extend to home community municipals when that community is a big city or county—even when you think you know quite a lot about city or county affairs. You may be able to assess the risk and reward possibilities very well when it comes to a small community—suburb, town, or rural county—in which you live. But the adjoining big city, the medium-sized city of half a million people, or the big county with hundreds of thousands of residents usually have such a large and diverse body of local problems and related regional, state, and federal funding problems as to defy your individual analysis. When you invest in the debt obligation of such a larger community, you must rely more upon the recommendations of bond-rating organizations than upon your personal knowledge.

The main need is to make that independent evaluation of the risk and your own informed buying decision. There is insurance now to cover some municipals, which can be helpful in the event of a default or a moratorium on interest payments—but it won't keep the value of the bond from falling disastrously if there is trouble, and it may not pay off if the failure is part of a much larger failure throughout the country. The tax advantage can be meaningful, even to small investors, though not as meaningful as to high-income people. And some municipals are relatively safe investments and likely to continue so, barring economic catastrophe. But with all that, municipals as a group are risky, so risky that it is vitally important to learn a good deal about the specific issuer and issue before you make the buying decision. *In municipals, there are no blue chips* as there are in corporate stocks and bonds; each issue must stand on its own feet and be fully understood. A New York City, Chicago, or Los Angeles municipal bond issue is not the equivalent of an IBM, Xerox, or General Motors stock or bond; the largest and best known of America's cities are often the riskiest municipal bond investments.

It is important to bear in mind continually that municipals and federal debt obligations carry entirely different kinds of risks. Federal obligations, backed by the federal government's unconditional promise to pay, are far safer than municipals. That is one of the reasons some sellers tout their wares confusingly as "governments"— without sharply differentiating between the several kinds of government obligations, as they should.

Some sellers also urge small investors not to "worry" about paying a premium for "good" municipals—that is, buying it a price higher than its face value—urging that the higher price paid only indicates how good an investment the municipal really is. Nonsense, of course; all bond prices fluctuate with interest rate fluctuations and the investment climate. A municipal selling for more than its face value, largely because it is thought by bond traders to be a relatively good risk, is simply a bond paying *a somewhat lower yield* than it did when issued. A bond, municipal or otherwise, paying $12 a year on its $100 face value, pays 12 percent. The same bond, bought at $105, with the same yearly payout, now pays 11.43 percent not 12 percent. When a broker tells you not to worry about something as obvious as that, it is time to worry about your broker.

Still, after all cautions have been duly noted, the tax-advantaged yields available can outweigh the risks, as long as you are extraordinarily careful about those risks and equally careful not to let your good judgment be overcome by a hard sell. And hard sells are often encountered in this part of the securities business. The compound interest tables continue to tell the story of opportunity best: A difference of just 2 points—2 percent—in after-tax yields, compounded over twenty years, becomes a very large difference indeed. Ten thousand dollars at an after-tax yield of 8 percent becomes $46,610 in twenty years. At an after-tax yield of 10 percent, the same $10,000 becomes $67,275 in twenty years. That is a difference of $20,665, or 44.23 percent—quite some difference.

KINDS OF MUNICIPALS

The kinds of municipals issued are similar to the kinds of corporate debt obligations discussed earlier. There are general obligations and defined ones; long-term obligations you can buy directly and short-term ones you can buy only through mutual funds.

General state and local (municipal) obligations are backed by the "full faith and credit" of their issuer, meaning that the issuer has made a bare promise to pay out of all available funds. The promise is unlimited, but is not backed by any revenues specifically dedicated to payment of interest and principal on the bond. It is backed by the taxing power of the government issuing the bond, but that's all that stands behind it—and it isn't necessarily very much. There is a huge difference between the unlimited promise to pay of the federal government and the unlimited promise to pay of another governmental body in the United States. The federal government promise is backed by unlimited taxing power, by the power to devalue currency, and ultimately by force, as necessary. Any other government has only the limited taxing power granted it by higher bodies. State taxing power is limited by the federal government; other bodies are limited by federal and state restrictions. This basic difference makes federal debt obligations as safe as obligations can be, while requiring investors to view all other government debt obligations very cautiously.

Nor does collateral stand behind government debt obligations, as it can behind private obligations. A city in default is not required by any kind of bankruptcy or other court to sell its assets to pay its creditors. It doesn't

work that way. The city keeps its assets, and the bondholders wait and hope—or sell at a small fraction of cost
and move on. Municipal bonds can be backed by specified revenues but are not collateralized in the same way
as private bonds.

Revenue bonds are those backed by specified revenues, as when a city or county builds a sports arena with
bond money and plans to pay interest and principal to
bondholders out of arena revenues. Such bonds are also
used to fund a wide variety of public works and business
development activities. Some revenue bonds can be sound
investments, but for small investors they pose something
of a problem within a problem, for it is often hard to get
a good view of the revenue prospects of the facility being
funded. If it is a new structure, as is so often the case,
it is often even harder to guess whether or not the structure will come in at or even near budget. Roads, bridges,
and especially nuclear power plants have been noto-
riously difficult to bring in anywhere near budget in recent years, with the result that those building them have
been forced to go to the public again and again for
additional funds—each time adding to the risks of bondholders by changing the anticipated equation of revenue-
to-money-invested for the facility. Nuclear power facilities, for example, have limited lives, and at the costs
many of these are incurring during building, it is very
hard to imagine that bondholders can reasonably expect
to get their money back from most of those now in construction or recently put into operation. On a considerably more catastrophic note, nuclear power bondholders
can also reasonably expect massive defaults and loss of
most of their money if they are imprudent enough to buy
nuclear bonds after the Washington State debacle and

the earlier Three Mile Island near disaster. This was once a promising industry; it may be so again, but now it is only a huge sink into which you should not pour any of your money.

But beside some of the revenue bonds issued in recent years, bridges and roads seem sane and very conservative. When a medium-sized one-industry town does a major refurbishing of its decaying midtown area in an attempt to attract more industry, it probably makes very good sense for the town. But for investors, it rarely makes any sense at all, for if no significant new industry is attracted—or if the deal that generated the whole refurbishing falls through, and the town's single main industry folds—then bondholders can kiss their money good-bye. Similarly, a revenue bond to fund an industrial park may be a project vitally necessary for a town, but if it does not attract enough tenants for long enough, bondholders will lose out.

Special assessment bonds are those funded out of taxes aimed at creating a specific improvement, for which local taxpayers are being specially taxed—that is, specially assessed—such as a local library building, dredging project, sewer system, or road. Like revenue bonds, they are as good as their sources of revenue are secure for the long term and each must be evaluated as a separate, possibly risky investment.

Special assessment bonds can provide excellent opportunities for making the kinds of municipal bond investments discussed earlier—very local, and triple tax exempt. The bonds of many affluent small communities carry far higher yields than should be expected, given the stability of the communities issuing them and the consequent safety of the bonds. That is because so many other municipals are so very risky in this period; the investment climate forces up the yields of these good bonds. That means unfortunately high interest payments for their issuers, and therefore higher taxes in those communities. It also creates investment opportunities for those wise enough to seek out and invest in such bonds.

As a small investor, you won't be able to make direct purchases of state and local short-term *tax-anticipation notes*, also called *warrants*, because they are issued only in very large denominations. These are bought by large institutions and are available only if you are invested in a mutual fund that holds them. Because they are short-term, ranging from as little as a few days to as long as six months, and because they are based on coming tax collections, fairly well determinable, they are safer than most other kinds of municipal obligations and relatively free from interest rate fluctuations. That is why institutions buy them, being far more cautious about the much riskier longer-term state and local debt obligations.

MUNICIPAL BOND FUNDS

There are also a large number of fiercely competitive, hard-selling municipal bond funds on the market. Some sell hard on the kind of triple tax exemption previously discussed. Others just sell hard, favorably comparing net after-tax yields with other forms of investment.

Many municipal bond funds make much of diversification, arguing that by spreading risks among many municipals you lessen the danger of serious harm caused by a single default. For example, an individual holding defaulted nuclear power bonds might lose all or almost all of the investment, while a bond fund might lose only a small portion of its total investment. That can be so.

If you are seriously considering an investment in municipals that you do not know intimately, you may be wise to consider municipal funds. On the other hand, it may be far better for small investors, who gain little from the tax advantages available in municipal bonds, not to invest in them at all, unless they are municipals they know a good deal about. That you may lose "only" 10 percent of your money on municipals in default, rather than all of it, is scarcely an inducement to invest at all. Bear in mind also that municipal bonds as a whole may be terribly vulnerable to the kind of scare caused by several defaults at once, and perfectly good bonds may then lose value in the market because of a general disenchantment with municipals. In that situation, municipal bond issuers will probably be forced, for at least some time, to issue bonds carrying higher interest rates—and the presence of those bonds in the market will drive down the value of other lower-interest municipals previously issued, including those you may hold as an individual or through a mutual fund.

THE TAX BREAK ON MUNICIPALS

Every municipal bond seller has a table of figures showing how much you are bound to make when you buy municipals, because of the huge tax savings available. Quite so. If you are in a combined top 50 percent income tax bracket, a municipal bond paying 9 percent will yield you somewhere around a real 18 percent on your money, depending upon whether you are filing singly or jointly and what the status of the tax law is that year. That's a lot, and in some instances can be well worth what may be limited risk.

But to be in a 50 percent bracket, you will probably have had to be making at least $40,000–$50,000 that year if you were single and at least $55,000–$65,000 if you were filing a joint return—probably considerably more, in both instances, for people with substantial incomes have usually taken some steps to shield their incomes from taxation, as through home purchase, IRAs, and Keogh plans. Bear in mind that municipal sellers are invariably talking about *taxable income*—that is, income after all deductions—rather than gross income.

More realistically, a small investor in an under-20 percent bracket can expect to add about 2 percentage points to the effective yield, give or take half a point, in periods in which the main body of municipal bond yields are in the 7–10 percent range. If you are in the 30 percent or so top bracket, figure about 4 points, again give or take about half a point. It starts getting interesting only in the 40 percent or so top bracket, where you can add 6 points or more. There, you begin to be able to see yields higher than those of blue-chip corporate bonds, which are generally far safer than most municipals. There, too, you begin to sees yields a few percentage points higher than those of federally insured bank certificates of deposit—if the risks don't bother you too much.

CHAPTER 7

Investing
in Mutual Funds

Mutual funds are much misunderstood by a great many small savers and investors. They are all too often thought to be safe investments, when in fact they span the whole range of risk, from funds that are relatively safe to those that are wildly speculative. They are often thought to be long-term investments, when in fact they are only as short- or long-term as what they are invested in, and must be watched just as closely every day as any other investment. People put their retirement money into speculative funds, pay huge sales charges when they need pay no charges at all, and in each major market fluctuation learn again that what goes up must come down, and that mutual funds are no exception to this rule.

When you put your money into a *mutual fund*, you are buying a share in a company that exists solely to invest the money of its shareholders, rather than to operate any other kind of business. Such a company is also called an *investment company*. The mutuality in the mutual fund is that there are many investors, all pooling their invested money and paying investment professionals to invest that money for them.

Some mutual funds, known as *closed-end* funds, consist of a fixed number of shares from the start, with their professional managers trying to increase the value of that starting investment. The only way to buy shares in that kind of investment company is to buy shares that have been sold by others and are therefore on the market. The main body of mutual funds, however, are known as *open-end* funds, because they consist of as many shares as their managers are able to sell, with more shares issued as sales are made.

Both open-end and closed-end mutual funds are as various as the kinds of investments they are in. Nothing in the basic closed- or open-end form determines the kinds of investments the fund will go into; that is purely a matter of fund management goals and market analyses as of the time that the money is being invested. Each mutual fund states its basic investment purposes clearly in its offering, written up in its prospectus, and generally stays with those stated purposes—but funds cover a wide range of investment objectives, and the funds available are therefore quite diverse.

HIGH-RISK FUNDS

One kind of mutual fund that becomes very popular when stocks are on their way up is the *equity fund*, which is a pool of shares in companies in which the fund has invested. A large equity fund may be invested in the shares of a hundred or more companies, in many industries. A kind of equity fund that is particularly popular in such periods is the *growth fund*, which is identified in prospectuses selling such funds much more correctly as a *high-risk fund*.

When you put your money into an equity fund, you are buying into a pool of stocks selected by the fund's managers, hoping that their professional judgment will be better than yours—and that by spreading your risks in a rising stock market you will be able to participate in that general rise, without being sunk by a few bad stock buys.

In a rising market, fund managers may indeed be able to bring in better value growths than you will on your own, even in the relatively nonspeculative equity funds, while also diversifying your risks. The problem is that in such a rising market the main "action" and investor buying attention is drawn to the high-risk funds, which are invested in whatever speculative stocks are being run up in any given period. In the 1960s, funds and individuals ran up several kinds of "glamour" stocks, which ran right down again in the 1970s. In the mid-1980s, funds and individuals ran up computer, other high technology, and bioengineering stocks, among others. Some of these have already begun to run down, as of this writing, being the stocks of small companies in very new industries. In any new industry, there may be very many promising small companies, but only a few will survive to become the IBMs and Xeroxes of the future. Most will fail, in an inevitable shakeout of the new industry.

Should you have any doubt at all as to how this works, look in the prospectuses of those equity mutual funds that are old enough to have fifteen years or more of history. As required by federal and state authorities, the fund's issuers have had to include some tremendously revealing figures. If you go enough years back, what you see is a roller coaster, with equity mutual funds reaching high levels in the mid-1960s, mirroring the booming markets of the time, and then dropping sharply in the

1970s, mirroring the declining markets of that time. In real dollar values, many have never made it back to the levels they reached twenty years ago, just as the stock market in which they are invested has not done so.

Do not pay too much attention to the "wonderful" recent records of high-risk growth funds. Believe their own prospectuses, which clearly label them as high risks, and be aware that if you put your money into such a fund, you are gambling on the stocks of a lot of very risky companies, rather than on anything like blue chips. You are also gambling on the ability of the fund's managers to pull fund money—your money—out of these high risks in a timely way when the glamour rubs off a little or when the whole market goes into decline, as it must from time to time. Unfortunately, the record of the high-risk mutual fund managers, as a group, is very bad in precisely these kinds of situations. Competitive pressure forces them to keep on pushing for high yields, while their stated purposes limit their ability to move your money into other kinds of investments, as you could—and should—do for yourself.

Beyond the high-risk equity funds, there are always other available ways to gamble in mutual funds, just as you can gamble by direct purchase of high risks. You can put your money into mutual funds heavily invested in precious metals and precious metals companies, even though these, like any commodities and commodity-based companies, are highly speculative investments. Or you can put your money into mutual funds based on foreign stocks, though any problems encountered in the United States will seem simple when compared with the problems encountered when investing abroad. In truth, you can be confident that whatever kind of high-risk investment is being widely sold will find its way into mutual fund form sooner or later. Use the same *extreme caution* when investing in mutual funds that you use when investing on your own.

INCOME FUNDS

But not all mutual funds involve high risks, any more than all investments do. Some bond-based funds can provide substantial income, with a diversified portfolio of medium- and long-term bonds affording considerable protection against fluctuations in individual bonds. This will certainly not protect you against fluctuations affecting the whole bond market, as when a general rise in interest rates forces down the values of existing bonds that have smaller yields than new bonds coming onto the market. But such funds, which often do heavily stress medium- and long-term federal and blue-chip corporate bonds can provide steady, sure income at fixed, predictable levels for as long as you hold them, and often at somewhat higher rates of return than money market mutual funds and bank money market funds.

MONEY MARKET
MUTUAL FUNDS

Money market mutual funds are very well known now, though they are actually quite a recent form, going back only to the 1970s. In that period, they became an alternative to the standard 5¼–5¾ percent savings account, paying so much more that eventually the banking industry successfully lobbied to be able to offer money market bank accounts, in competition with mutual funds.

Money market mutual funds are pools of money invested wholly in short-term debt obligations, with no obligation longer than one year and average obligations in the 90–120 day range. They are very sensitive to interest rate changes, as they are invested heavily in quite short-term obligations, such as overnight loans to banks, short-term Treasury bills, large-denomination short-term corporate paper, and short-term bank CDs. Some of these funds invest in the whole available range of short-term obligations, while others limit their investments—as, for example, to federal government obligations. These funds are not federally insured. However, those funds wholly in federal obligations are, in effect, fully protected by government guarantees of its own debt obligations; that is just as good as the federal guarantee of bank deposits.

Although not federally insured, many money market mutual funds have in recent years provided private insurance of their assets, as a means of competing with banks offering federally insured bank accounts. *Caution*: That private insurance may be excellent as to individual mutual fund defaults, but in the event of economic catastrophe, it cannot properly be relied upon. No private companies are really strong enough to insure funds against that kind of economic collapse, and it is only in that kind of situation that such funds are likely to get into trouble.

These money market mutual funds stay quite short-term, are quite able to hold their value and meet any "run on the bank" by shareholders, and—short of catastrophe—are very safe and very good investments. They should be watched, of course, as should all investments; catastrophes can occur, and there may come a time when you want to take some or all of your funds out of the financial marketplace for a time.

Money market mutual funds do have some advantages over bank accounts, in that most carry no-cost checking privileges and other no-cost and low-cost services. However, when linked up with a brokerage asset management account, you may find that the cost of brokerage trades outweighs the other advantages. Comparative shopping is very much in order here, as throughout the financial marketplace.

BALANCED FUNDS AND FAMILIES OF FUNDS

Investment managers running mutual funds that are dedicated to narrow purposes, such as growth or income, cannot be expected to steer you out of their funds when they are no longer really appropriate for your goals or in the current investment climate. As a practical matter, the managers of a growth fund may try to put the fund into a defensive position when the stock market breaks sharply downward for a long period, but they will not tell their investors to get out of stocks altogether while the getting is good and move their money into bonds and money market instruments.

In the 1960s, the main device the mutual fund industry developed to cope with swings in the investment situation was the *balanced fund*, which invested in several kinds of instruments, moving money back and forth as the investment situation changed. In the 1980s many large balanced funds remain, joined now by the *family of funds* arrangement, in which one management and sales organization will have a substantial series of different kinds of funds all under one investment roof. Fund shareholders are then enabled to move their money back and forth, essentially at will, and with little or no additional selling and transaction charges, as they move from fund to fund within a family.

You still have to watch your investments, and make money moving decisions that you might have expected professional fund managers to be able to make for you, but that is no real change. Entirely contrary to the selling talk and technique of the mutual fund industry, it is quite wrong to think of mutual funds as long-term investments, which you somehow have to watch less carefully than other investments because professionals are managing your money for you. Far from it. The worst error that mutual fund shareholders consistently make is to hold on to mutual funds far too long, because they have paid far too little attention to their fund shareholdings. Small investors, and particularly small mutual fund investors, habitually buy late and high, holding too long and selling late for too little. Mutual funds are just as volatile as any other investments and have to be watched just as hard.

MUTUAL FUND
CHARGES AND FEES

Because your money in mutual funds does have to be watched carefully and moved as quickly as necessary, it is crucially important to keep fees of all kinds down. You may not have to pay much for a transfer of money between funds in the same family, but if you have to pay 8.5 percent of your invested money to get into the fund, 0.5 percent yearly management fee, 1 percent yearly marketing fee, and 4 percent of invested money fee to get out in the first year of the investment, your freedom of selling action is severely limited and your profit possibilities are minimal, to put it very gently. No, you aren't likely to have to pay all that to a single fund in a single year, but all those charges are present in the industry, and there are circumstances in which they could all come together.

The *front-load* charge is by far the worst thing that the mutual fund industry does to its investors. Until the advent of hard-selling, heavily advertised *no-load* funds, many investors didn't even know they had a choice, and paid what they thought was a standard 8 percent or 8.5 percent of invested money as a sales charge to mutual funds in which they invested.

Paying an 8.5 percent front-load charge means that if you invest $10,000 in a mutual fund with such a charge, $850 is taken right off the top of your money as soon as you buy into the fund. The day you start, your money has shrunk to $9,150, and to get back up to your original $10,000 you have to make $850 on a base of $9,150, or 9.28 percent. If you decide to sell out your mutual fund the day after you buy into it, that $850 is gone. Contrast that with a discount broker's stock transaction charge of perhaps $50–$100, and you get some idea of the magnitude of the cost. Contrast that with the zero cost of buying into a no-load fund, which will be just as fully and well managed as the front-loading fund, and the foolishness of buying into a front-loaded fund becomes apparent. *The main reason that mutual fund sellers push front-loaded funds is that they get higher commissions from those sales than from no-load fund sales.* That 8.5 percent goes to pay for selling costs *and has nothing at all to do with fund management.*

Paying that 8.5 percent right off the top is entirely wasteful, from the investor's point of view. Equally bad is that paying it tends to rob you of your freedom and flexibility as to investment decisions. In a rapidly chang-

ing investment climate, you may indeed need to move
your money quickly out of a fund, and the immediate
loss of the front-load money may stop you from making
the right decision.

Management fees are an entirely different matter.
You have to be ready to pay for professional management,
and the ¼–¾ percent of fund assets that are charged
as management fees yearly should be seen as normal and
acceptable. Every fund must charge for management; it
is the selling costs that can be onerous and unacceptable.

As the mutual fund industry becomes more and more
competitive, selling costs continue to rise. Many mutual
funds are now charging as much as 1 percent of fund
assets yearly on top of all other selling and management
costs, for additional selling costs. That may not sound
like much, but when it goes on year after year it can be
a substantial drain on a fund's assets and rob you of an
important part of your compounded growth.

Many funds are also beginning to charge *back loads*,
that is, a charge of as much as 4 percent for taking your
money out of a fund before a specified time. This is
usually a sliding scale arrangement, as when the fund
charges you 1 percent less each year until the fourth year
and no charge at all for getting out after that. This too
is both a very serious penalty and a powerful impediment
to making the right investment decisions at the right
times.

A good many formerly no-load funds are beginning
to charge front loads, usually in the 2–3 percent range,
as their selling costs go up. Unfortunately, advertising
costs money, and if the only way to attract new investors
is to advertise competitively, then that must be done. For
that reason, it may not be possible for very much longer
to take the view that no investor should pay any kind of

front load when buying a mutual fund. On the other hand, competitive pressures also mean that there will probably continue to be a good number of *no-load* funds still available and reachable, as before, very easily through your response to newspaper ads. There is a new way to reach no-load funds, as well; some discount brokers now advertise that they will supply lists of no-load funds for their investors. Between the ads and the discount brokers, it should not be hard to find the kinds of mutual funds you want. You should buy into a front-loaded fund only if you have become convinced that that particular fund is an especially good investment and you are willing to pay that high front-load sales charge for the privilege of getting into it. Otherwise, there is no reason to do so and every reason to buy into a no-load or very low-load fund.

CHAPTER 8

Gold and Other Precious Goods

The question of investing in gold is always there. In stable, prosperous times gold as an investment is pushed considerably into the background. In bad or even only uncertain times, gold very quickly comes to the fore as an investment vehicle. That is all quite understandable. Even now, when gold is neither used as money nor backs the money of any major nation in the world, it is still viewed by people all over the world as an ultimate store of value. Even in modern industrial nations, like the United States, Britain, and France, people hoard gold, in bank vaults, in attics and cellars, and in the traditional hole in the ground in the backyard or out somewhere in the fields. And for those in such unstable areas as the Mideast, gold continues to be bought, hoarded, and placed in safe storage abroad as a matter of ordinary good sense. There is even a whole school of thought that insists gold is the only finally reliable store of value, because through either inflation or outright repudiation governments always fail to pay their debts, while gold keeps and even adds to its value in the long run, no matter what else happens.

Yet in the kind of crisis in which the United States and other major industrial nations would indeed fail to pay their debts—which would be the kind of crisis brought on by nuclear war or so deep a worldwide depression as to bring economic breakdown throughout the world— even gold probably would not do. Then it would have to be survival supplies—guns, canned goods, water, and the rest—rather than any medium of exchange, including gold. Short of that kind of crisis, United States government promises to pay should hold, and backyard gold hoards seem mainly unnecessary.

GOLD AS AN INVESTMENT

Seeing gold as an investment, rather than as a survival need, means understanding how it behaves in the financial marketplace and comparing it with other ways in which you can use your saving and investing money. For, while gold does tend to hold its value and is therefore in that sense a very safe investment, there are some real problems connected with it as an investment, whether you buy it as bullion, coins, mining stocks, stock-based mutual funds, or very highly speculative futures.

If you buy gold and hold it for decades, you will probably come out with something like the real dollars you put in at the start, minus any capital-gains taxes you paid at the end. You will also have had a store of value that was as safe as a federally insured bank account. Those two characteristics together might have been extraordinarily attractive when the rate of inflation was so high and the rate of return on safe personal savings and investments so low that it was almost impossible to keep up with the inflation rate, and all savings seemed to melt away in real dollars year by year. But that is not true in this period. Now there are several good ways to beat the inflation rate and make real dollar gains with your money. That is the basic reason gold should not be attractive now to small savers and investors.

Gold just sits there, paying no interest or dividends. If you start a year with an ounce of gold worth $400 and you end the year with that ounce still worth $400, you have in one sense held your money intact. But if in that year you could have had an after-tax yield of 10 percent, what you lost was that 10 percent, which is worth $40. And you will lose the compounding on that money and all the other compoundings in other years, as long as you hold the gold and it does nothing but sit there. That 10 percent is realistic, by the way, as gold should properly be seen as a very long-term kind of investment for small investors, and yield should therefore be compared to the kinds of yields you can get from money put into tax-advantaged IRAs.

It would be somewhat different if you could count on gold to do, year by year, what it can be pretty well counted on to do in the long run—that is, to hold its value in real dollars. If the rate of inflation was 7 percent and gold could be counted on to go up by 7 percent along with the rate of inflation, then you would be losing 3 percent of the 10 percent you could have made, still a real loss but a much smaller one. And in some years, inflation might outstrip possible yield, evening things up a bit. But unfortunately that's not the way it works. In any given year, or in any group of years, gold may stay right where it is or even lose some of its market value, causing you large losses in forgone income, loss of compounded interest, and even direct dollar losses if you are forced to sell.

All that is because gold is something beyond being a safe store of value. It is a commodity, as well. That means it fluctuates in market value, behaving essentially just like all other commodities. It is subject to supply and demand factors, to the impact of speculation, and to the general economic climate. The truth is that if you buy gold, you had better be prepared either to hold it for a very long time, through all kinds of fluctuations, or to treat it as the speculation it really is in the short term.

Gold has fluctuated a great deal in recent years. When Americans were finally allowed to buy it legally and price controls on it were lifted, you could have bought some for $35 an ounce, watched it stay at or near that price, just sitting there, and then sold it within a year, reasoning that it was just a bad buy. If, however, you had held it for a few years, you would have seen it take an enormous run up into the $800 per ounce range, well over twenty times what you paid for it. But if you had bought it in the $800 per ounce range—as so many small investors did, coming in late and buying at the top—you then might have held on for years more and watched your gold lose half its dollar value while yielding nothing at all. At this writing, gold is selling in the $400 per ounce range.

Supply and demand has a good deal to do with gold prices. Much of the world's gold in the ground is in South Africa and the Soviet Union. A good deal more is in the hands of the world's governments, especially that of the United States, which hold gold as a backup store of value. Some is in the hands of international banking organizations. A good deal of it—nobody really knows how much—is in the ground in a different way, buried there by private citizens hoarding gold. The rest is traded as a store of value or used for industrial purposes, and there is not terribly much of it, compared to what is otherwise held. Therefore, it is possible for the Soviet Union, South Africa, the United States, or any of several other major holders to have an enormous effect on the short-term price of gold by dumping gold stocks on the world market to raise funds for other purposes—or, for that matter, as an instrument of competitive international policy.

In the short term, speculation can also have a great deal to do with gold prices. As gold prices begin to move, even a little, large international traders can be counted on to speculate in the thin gold supplies available for trading.

General political and economic conditions can have a very powerful influence on the market price of gold. For sound reasons or not, the fact is that, when times are very uncertain, many people around the world buy and hoard gold, creating powerful upward pressure on its market price. In many instances, that is just good common sense. Those living in countries with enormous rates of inflation and very weak governments are wise to do anything they can to acquire and hold safe stores of value, if possible outside their own countries. In some instances, it is just panic, as it was in the United States in the mid-1970s. On the other hand, it is entirely un-derstandable that people with living memories of the Great Depression of the 1930s and of World War II might become nervous in difficult times and hoard gold.

It is often very tempting to speculate when market prices are skyrocketing. It is particularly tempting when gold is involved, for then it is easy to rationalize the speculation, telling yourself that somehow you "can't lose," because gold really holds its value, anyway. Well, everything said above shows that to be untrue. Gold holds its value only in the very long run. In the short run, it is as risky and dangerous a speculation as any other, and small investors who speculate in gold in competition with gold traders all around the world are quite likely to lose their shirts.

An indirect way to buy into gold is to purchase stock in companies whose main business is gold mining, whether you do so directly or through mutual funds focusing on gold mining stocks. Many gold mining stocks and mutual funds based on them have done extremely well in recent years, especially when gold prices have been flying high.

But what goes up can come down, and gold mining stocks and mutual funds are really as speculative as the value of the gold supporting them. When gold rises, they rise; when gold prices tumble, so do gold stocks. There is a little more stability in the stocks of well-established companies sitting on piles of gold in the ground than in speculation based on the current price of gold, but not enough to change what is, for small investors, the undesirable speculation involved.

Caution: South African gold mining stocks are often highly touted by stock market analysts specializing in gold and other precious metals. However, South African political conditions add a very large element of uncertainty to the long-term prospects of South African mining companies. No matter how stable the situation in southern Africa seems at any given moment, it would be wise to bear in mind that any large additional element of uncertainty, even far short of revolution and expropriation of mining companies, is likely to drive South African mining company stock far, far down. Then, no matter how much gold there is in the ground, you may have to sell your stock at a huge loss.

You can also buy gold as "futures"; those will be discussed in the next chapter.

OTHER PRECIOUS METALS

For small investors, other precious metals are more obviously speculations. Silver, platinum, and uranium are not really commodities that you are going to purchase and hold against the threats of runaway inflation, worldwide depression, and nuclear war. So, too, for a variety of "strategic metals," such as manganese and molybdenum, which have been recommended by some in the last few years as appropriate "hard goods" investments for uncertain times.

You can buy silver much as you can buy gold—as bars, coins, stocks, mutual funds, or very highly speculative futures. The other metals can be bought in all these ways, but are not used in coinage. The main thing to bear in mind about them is that, with the exception of silver bars and coins, none are the kinds of commodities that would in any way be useful in the event of economic collapse or nuclear war. For industrial companies using them, these are necessary commodities and bought and traded as such. For professional traders and speculators, these are the stuff of day-to-day work. But for small, amateur, quite unknowing investors, these are purely gambles. Look with great skepticism upon any investment seller or adviser who wants to take you into this sort of thing. Bear in mind that, if you do go in, you are unlikely to be able to learn enough to get to know what you are doing. These kinds of fast, complex games are really not for amateurs.

GEMSTONES

Diamonds, sapphires, rubies, and many other gemstones have for thousands of years and all over the world been highly prized as stones of value. They are small, very valuable, and therefore entirely portable. They have in many times and places been hidden and smuggled from place to place and have provided the basis for new lives and fortunes.

In that sense, like gold, they have great residual value and are unlikely in the long run to lose that value. But, like gold, they are also commodities that fluctuate in price with supply and demand, speculation, and general economic and political conditions.

They are less easily tradable than gold, however, and this can be a substantial drawback. When you hold gemstones, you may not easily be able to find markets for them, and your gemstones will not necessarily command fixed prices, as do commodities that are traded in more highly organized markets. Instead, you may find yourself bargaining with professionals in markets in which you have little expert knowledge, for goods that are really very hard to value precisely.

Because of these kinds of valuation and market price uncertainties, gemstones have been particularly vulnerable to fraudulent selling practices. A classic of its kind was the fraud involving the sale of gemstones in sealed packets, which were not to be opened by their purchasers because that would void their "guarantees" of purity and value. Nonsense, of course. Yet thousands of small investors were successfully defrauded before the scam was exposed. Fraud aside, though, gemstones are quite hard to value and difficult to sell easily when you want to.

During the 1970s and early 1980s, gemstones became objects of considerable speculation, with buying pressure therefore forcing prices up quite unrealistically. As soon as the terribly adverse and uncertain markets and economic conditions of that period eased a little, gemstone prices declined very sharply, and hundreds of thousands of gemstone holders lost substantial portions of their invested money. Then the nature of the speculation was clearly seen—but too late to help the losers. That is why gemstones are very unpopular at this writing.

But that will change. Just as those who today invest in highly speculative growth mutual funds have forgotten the lessons of the 1960s, so some investors in the future will forget the gemstone debacle of the 1980s. And as always, some gemstones are good buys today, when they are unpopular and relatively low-priced. The wise small investor will not stay away from gemstones because they are gemstones, but will rather take the trouble to learn enough about them to be able to look astutely for substantial values in a down market, planning to sell when the market rises.

COLLECTIBLES

That is also how collectibles should be viewed—except that your own very special knowledge, in a field in which you have become an expert collector, may cause you to hold on to some items for decades, through rises and declines. As of this writing, collectibles as a class of investments have become quite unpopular with small investors, while at the same time specific kinds of things collected continue to grow in value very nicely and to be collected by the knowing.

Collectibles are any tangible items that are in limited supply or will one day be in limited supply, for which at least an informal trading market exists, if only through the classified ad columns of special-interest magazines. You can stretch that even a little further and include items for which you have become convinced that a market will later exist, even if one does not now exist. People collect and trade all kinds of things, from paintings and ceramics worth millions of dollars each to matchboxes and comic books only a few decades old, which may be worth as little as a few dollars to a few thousand dollars on their markets. You need only go to a large flea market on a summer Sunday to see small machine-made glass dishes, which were turned out by the millions, selling individually for far more than they were originally worth, or to see sheet music from the turn of the century selling for as many dollars as the few pennies for which it originally sold.

As disillusioned small investors moved away from common stocks into hard goods during the 1970s, they began to buy all kinds of such items. As the years went by and markets developed, they bought on balance far more than they sold, constantly pushing prices up on all sorts of likely and quite unlikely collectibles, most of them with little or no underlying or long-term collecting value. Late in the period, a real wave of speculation developed, fueled by seeming gains in value across the board—though these were, for most, only gains on paper, as the items were usually held for anticipated further appreciation in value. This kind of speculation was also fueled by some professional sellers, who found it enormously lucrative to go into the mass sale of collectibles by mail. For example, millions of people bought newly made "limited editions" of items made of silver or gold—though sometimes only plated with those substances or even made of stainless steel—thinking that they were investing in collectibles. Hundreds of thousands and perhaps millions more bought limited editions of lithographs and other artworks—though some were merely mechanical reproductions, rather than real limited-edition lithographs—on the same theory. The promoters of these goods did not directly claim they would go up in value; the laws prohibits that kind of claim. They did hint at it, though, and word of mouth among gullible small investors did the rest. Everything did go up, and fast. Ultimately, as is so easy to see now, the plates and the rest of the precious metal items turned out to be worth only as much as their underlying metal content was worth on the open market, after deducting the cost of melting them down. Much of the rest turned out to be worthless junk. Only those items that had real collecting interest before and after the speculative fads had run their course continued to hold and grow in value.

But this is not a caution against investing in collectibles. Far from it. It is only a caution against investing in collectibles that you know nothing about—quite the same as advice not to invest in unknown high-flying stocks or put your money into other high-risk speculations only because some eager stockbroker urged you to do so. If you are a hobbyist collector, who keeps up closely with values as they develop in your field or fields of interest, you may be able to develop extremely high-yield collections, buying and selling every step of the way and ultimately using your collections to fund much of your later-years money needs and as a legacy to your heirs. That happened to many stamp and coin collectors, who continued to follow their interests all during the decades before their hobbies became fashionable investments. It

continues to happen when people carefully and knowl-
edgeably collect books, guns, prints, and a score of other
items, for which well-established formal and informal
evaluation channels and trading markets exist. Do collect, if you have a bent in that direction; you can make
money at it and even turn it into a later-years part-time
occupation, if you want to, as so many others have done.

CHAPTER 9

Other
Speculations

As discussed in Chapter 8, several kinds of valuable goods
can be both stores of value and speculations, depending
upon how they are seen and used by investors. But some
of the forms in which they and other tangibles and intangibles can be invested are purely speculative, and they
are the topic of this chapter. It is really not enough to
view investments in futures, stock options, and some tax
shelters cautiously and very skeptically. The pressure to
speculate can be very strong, and friends and sellers can
be very persuasive; it is important to know how these
speculations work, so that you can make informed judgments about whether or not to participate.

FUTURES: WHAT THEY ARE
AND HOW THEY WORK

A future is a uniform contract to buy or sell a specific
quantity of items of value, whether tangible or intangible,
at some fixed future time, usually within one year. These
uniform contracts specify quantities of items, quality, and

the terms of the trade, and each contract is identical with all other contracts of the same kind, as bought and sold on organized exchanges. When you trade in futures, what you are trading is these contracts themselves, rather than the commodities or intangibles covered by the contracts.

At this writing, trading in futures—and in futures options—is actively conducted on several American commodity exchanges, and you can speculate in futures and options in a very wide range of metals, livestock, foods, industrial products, financial instruments, and even stock indexes. This has become quite a gambling game.

There are some underlying real markets here, on which the speculative futures markets have grown. A worldwide set of commodity markets exists, in which companies must buy both for current use and future needs, attempting to plan production and pricing on the basis of known future supply prices. Therefore, two kinds of prices have developed in these world markets—the *spot price*, which is for commodities actually changing hands when traded, and the *future price*, which is the price that will be paid later, with no commodities actually changing hands until then.

Users buying futures do so to hold supplies at predictable prices for future use; they seldom speculate in futures. But futures prices do continually change, and speculators buying futures trade large quantities of goods on paper in order to try to win large gains—usually on borrowed money in margin accounts. The rules of those exchanges on which futures are traded limit the size of price changes that can occur in a single trading day, but futures contracts are so large that even small price changes can enable a trader, on a single day, to make substantial gains—or losses.

These large contracts are clearly geared to the needs

of industrial users. No individual investor-speculator is going to take delivery on a contract calling for the purchase of 10 tons of cocoa, 5,000 bushels of oats, 125,000 West German marks, or 25,000 pounds of copper. For individual investors, this is purely a gambler's set of markets, developed on top of a set of markets that meet economic needs.

FUTURES OPTIONS

Speculators also trade in futures options. Such an option is the right to buy or sell at a stated price within a stated time. By speculating in options on futures contracts, rather than on the futures contracts themselves, they enormously increase their possible risks and possible rewards. And if they do it with borrowed money, in a margin account, they can increase their possible gains and losses even more.

Any tradable option, including traded commodity purchase and sale options, is itself a legally enforceable contract and something of value. Those investors who buy options are usually betting that the prices of those contracts optioned will go up and that the option then will be profitably exercised. Those who sell think the prices will go down and that the options will not be exercised, as they would be for higher prices than then-current selling prices.

Futures options, then, pyramid an additional gamble on top of a gamble. The theory is that if you hold an option on a futures contract that has gone up, you can multiply your profits with very small amounts of cash actually invested. If you hold an option on a futures contract that has gone down, you need not exercise the option and have lost only the small amount you have paid for the option. This is only theory, of course. What really happens is that small investors often get carried away. They take a little gamble today, plus slightly larger gambles tomorrow and the day after—"just to catch up"—and can end up losing everything they put in. These markets move fast, and losses can pile up very quickly.

Small investors can also make some money fast, which is worse. Then the amateur tends to put in more and ultimately loses more. Small investors have very little chance of coming out of futures and futures options gambles unscathed. In any crowd of small futures and options investors, you can count the number of long-run winners on the fingers of one hand.

INVESTING IN FUTURES AND FUTURES OPTIONS

Brokers like futures and options trading very much, given the size of the commissions generated. Because these are such fast in-and-out markets, they require very many trading transactions, with traders often taking *day trading* positions—that is, closing positions each night to prevent losses from overnight price swings. That, in turn, means a trade at night and a trade the next morning, with each trade generating new commissions. In the course of a single year, it is not at all unusual for trading commissions to exceed the total amount of money a trader has invested in cash in the futures and options trading account. There have even been some spectacular cases, in which the trading positions in futures options were so large and were traded so actively that the commissions generated far exceeded the total amounts in the account, even when the whole account was in the process of being lost. Nor can you really control the number of trades in your account, as the pace of trading is so fast that most brokers insist on being granted full or partial discretionary trading powers.

Very few small investors really trade futures and options on their own. As a practical matter, they trade either through brokers or professional advisers who guide their trades, or in groups through futures mutual funds or in investment clubs. If you do decide to plunge into speculation in this fashion, you are probably best advised to do so either through a fund or a club, to avoid the otherwise extraordinarily high cost of doing this kind of business through a broker. Nor should you count on using a discount broker in this area, as this is one kind of trading in which the small investor really does need professional guidance. *No matter how you trade, though, the cards are very much stacked against the small investor in futures and futures options trading.*

STOCK OPTIONS

Stock options can be a little different, though these too are in the main properly seen as speculations.

The kind of stock option that is tradable is not the kind that an employee gets, which is to buy company stock at a specified price within a specified period. That kind of stock option can only be used by the employee and is therefore not tradable.

A tradable option to buy specified stock at a fixed price within a specified time is a *call*. A tradable option to sell, rather than to buy, is a *put*. When it is an option to buy more shares at a fixed price within a specified time and is attached to a new stock issue, it is a *right*. And when it is an option to buy more bonds or preferred shares and is attached to a new bond or preferred share issue, it is a *warrant*. All are rather easily confused, but all are different kinds of stock options and are quite different from futures options. All four kinds of stock options are tradable up to the dates on which they expire, and all have value, in and of themselves, until they expire.

When you trade in puts and calls, you are trading in stock options. The *put*, or option to sell, is a bet that the price of the stock will go down more than the difference between the cost of the put and its current market value. Then, sale at the fixed price set in the put will be sale at a profit, and the speculation will have succeeded. But if the stock does not go down, or even goes up, the cost of the put will be lost. On the other hand, many traders, when buying such a put, hedge against a sharp drop by simultaneously buying a call; then, if the stock does go down sharply, they are able to sell at not-too-ruinous a loss.

The call buyer takes the opposite view and is betting that the stock's price will rise more than the difference between the price of the call and the stock's current market price. If it does, the call owner will be able to buy at then-lower-than-market prices and resell at a profit. If not, all or some of the price of the call will be lost.

Used as a hedge to limit risk, rather than as speculation, trading in puts and calls is a reasonable tactic for professional stock traders and sometimes even for small investors. The nearly simultaneous buying of puts and calls—the technique called the *straddle*—is also useful for risk-hedging by professionals, but amateurs should try it only with a little professional help, at least the first few times.

TAX-SHELTERED
SPECULATIONS

In the past few decades, a considerable commerce has built up in investments known as *tax shelters*—that is, investments designed to take advantage of the American tax system's multifold opportunities to join investment to tax advantage and thus produce high after-tax yields. At this writing—though this will change with new laws, regulations, and judicial decisions, perhaps by the time you read this page—some popular tax-sheltered investments are in real estate, oil and gas exploration and production, coal production, and equipment leasing, with less popular but still-used tax shelters in such investments as cattle and research and development programs. As loopholes close and old tax shelters can no longer be used, new loopholes and accompanying new tax-shelter opportunities become available. It is pointless to analyze specific tax shelters here, in a fast-changing legal situation, but it is sensible to comment on them in general as investment opportunities for small savers and investors.

The most general and appropriate comment of them all is that the above are not at all the only tax shelters around; nor are they the most appropriate for small investors. Everything that has gone before in this book should make that clear. For small investors, IRAs and Keogh plans are the best tax shelters of them all. Municipals are also prime tax shelters—as long as you know what you are doing. Annuities, which will be discussed in Chapter 10, are by their nature also very considerably tax-sheltered. For small investors, all these may be far better than many of the tax shelters sold by the tax-shelter portion of the financial industry.

If you do seriously consider going into one of the kinds of investments called tax shelters, the main question to ask is whether you believe it would be a sound investment *without* its tax-shelter aspects. And that is the key question, for it is all too easy to be blinded by tax advantage and possible after-tax yield, and to lose sight of the huge inherent risks in some kinds of tax-sheltered investments.

Not all. Some producing oil, gas, and coal properties may be sound enough, though not always attractive enough for small investors in terms of after-tax yield. But some may be terribly risky. And some tax shelters should be clearly seen as investments small investors should not go into at all. For example, it really doesn't matter how tax-advantaged or potentially profitable an oil or gas exploration venture may be. It may also turn out to be a dry hole or series of dry holes in the ground, producing nothing and losing all the money put into it.

Mutual funds investing in many of these kinds of tax shelters may spread the risks a little, but essentially they share in those inherent risks. At this moment, I am looking at a rather typical prospectus in this area, which announces organization of a mutual fund for the purpose of buying properties producing oil and gas. The fund has no track record at all, no properties are specified, there are substantial start-up costs, and the key people are almost all very young. Further, the prospectus clearly states that there will be no ready market for fund shares, that you may not be able to transfer shares even if you can find a buyer, and that under certain conditions your limited liability as a limited partner may turn out to be unlimited. Many other risks are also stated. On the face of it, no small investor should buy into this fund, and larger investors should be almost equally wary, regardless of the tax advantages involved. Yet many large and small investors will buy, blinded by the seeming tax advantages and by the marketing power of the reputable firm selling it.

Go for tax advantage, by all means and in all the safe ways discussed in this and other chapters of this book. But beware of speculative tax shelters.

CHAPTER 10

Insurance as an Investment

In the widest sense, life, health, liability, and property insurance are all essential parts of financial planning. But because this book is concerned somewhat more narrowly with savings and investment matters, it is in that context that insurance is discussed here, for some kinds of life insurance and annuity policies have historically been and still are major forms used by small savers and investors.

Until very recently, with the introduction of somewhat higher-yielding policies, the use of insurance policies as savings and investment vehicles by millions of small investors has been little more than a tribute to the aggressive and very successful selling tactics of the major life insurance companies. For many decades, the savings component in life insurance and annuity policies paid less than did many other equally safe investments. It was sheer ignorance on the part of insurance buyers that allowed life insurance companies to make enormous profits and their insureds' invested money, while paying as little as 2–3 percent in actual yield. The spread between insurance company returns on invested money and what was credited to those insured was so great that the companies could even afford to pay front loads to their sales-

people on regular life insurance policies—usually
amounting to the whole first year's premium payments—
and still make tremendous profits in the long run. For
certain kinds of policies, that situation has changed very
little, and for others only moderately, even now. *The
main thing to do when considering an insurance purchase
is to separate the investment yield questions from the insurance questions. Only then can you make good decisions.* For most of our lives, we need life insurance to
protect our loved ones, but that needed life insurance
can be bought with or without an investment component.

Note also that a major tax-saving aspect of life insurance has changed in this period. When estate taxes
affected even rather small estates, the fact that life insurance proceeds passed tax-free to heirs was quite meaningful for estate planning purposes, even to people of
relatively modest means. But now a married couple can,
on the death of one spouse, claim a $250,000 nontaxable
marital deduction for estate tax purposes. Today, not
many small savers and investors have to worry about estate
taxes and can instead focus on maximizing after-tax yields
during their lifetimes. For most, that means buying term
insurance to meet life insurance needs, and putting investment money into better investments than regular life
insurance policies.

TERM LIFE INSURANCE

The basic life insurance transaction between the insured
and the company involves the payment of premiums by
the insured and death benefits by the insurance company,
the amount of those premiums being based on compu-
tation of average life expectancies, plus an allowance for

insurance company costs and profits. This basic transaction does not include savings and investment features, which are entirely unnecessary for insurance purposes.

Term insurance is the kind of life insurance that results from the basic insurance transaction. The purchaser of term insurance buys a guarantee that the insurance company will pay a specified amount of insurance to beneficiaries on his or her death in return for premium payments. Those payments are for a specific number of years and at specific rates; these depend on the age of the insured, with rates on term policies usually rising as the insured ages. The insured can cancel the policy at any time, but the insurance company cannot, unless premium payments stop.

Term insurance is by far the least expensive kind of life insurance available, the premiums often being only a small fraction of what would have to be paid on regular life policies, for the same size death benefits (with investment components). That is especially so for younger people, especially those with small children; for them the difference in necessary premium payments can often mean the difference between having as much insurance as they really need and being pathetically underinsured. There are several slightly different kinds of term policies; all are very easily explored with any of tens of thousands of eager insurance agents.

Group policies, such as those with which employers cover employees, are almost always term policies. But they often are hard to convert to affordable insurance when leaving a job, and you should certainly always have an independent term insurance policy of your own, aside from employment coverage. That kind of coverage is often inexpensively available as savings bank life insurance, or through religious, fraternal, or alumni organizations. Some life insurance is also attached to mortgage and other loans, but this diminishes as the loans are repaid and should not be counted on for long-term protection. As the "financial marketplace" concept continues to be actively pressed by all kinds of financial industry organizations, life insurance, including its term insurance variety, is also increasingly available from mutual funds and commercial banks.

WHOLE LIFE INSURANCE

In many millions of life insurance policies, the investment portion of the policy is added on top of the life insurance itself. These are the policies called *whole life, permanent life, straight life,* or *regular life,* all of which mean exactly the same thing. To them has recently been added *universal life,* which tends to pay somewhat higher rates of yield and is highly touted by insurance sellers as something very new, but is—in essence—just like the other high-premium-paying, high-commission-paying life insurance policies.

Don't be fooled by the differing names of all these insurance policies and by the claims of their sellers. These policies all build up an investment fund in your policy by applying some of your high premium payments to that fund and the balance to the real life insurance in the policy, which pays death benefits, just like term insurance. Aside from that, the only significant difference is that your premiums for these kinds of policies are usually level, that is the same each year, instead of graduating as you age. This means that it is harder and harder to cost-justify a change of policies once you are a few years into a particular policy, a fact that works very much to the advantage of the insurance company.

Many people are attracted by the ability to borrow at low interest rates from their own insurance policy investment funds and by the ability to skip premium payments by taking the money from their own accumulated policy funds. And you can. You have the "privilege" of borrowing your own money, usually at somewhere around 8 percent as of this writing.

That money will have been growing in most policies at pathetically low rates of return. Some insurance companies—who have been making as much as 15–18 percent on insureds' money—have been crediting existing whole-life contracts with somewhat higher yields in this high-interest period, but still only in the 5–7 percent range, while much higher and even safer yields were available elsewhere. And the investment funds in some existing policies still continue to be credited only in the 3–5 percent range. From an investment point of view, it makes no sense at all to buy a whole-life insurance policy, and there seems little reason to do so even from a life insurance point of view.

As competition for investors' money grows in the financial marketplace, higher yields on life insurance policy investment funds are being offered by many companies. When high enough—for example in the 9–11 percent range as of this writing—their combination of tax advantage and yield can make them attractive for estate planning purposes. But that is a very limited plus for small savers and investors, who must try hard to maximize investment returns for very real lifetime needs of their own, during uncertain times. If you made the mistake of putting your money into a whole-life policy, by

all means consider borrowing the money in the policy
back—unless the interest rate is too high—and putting
it into higher-yielding investments that will be available
to you when you want the money, or when you see the
desirability of moving the money about for greater yield.
And if you are considering the purchase of a new life
insurance policy, buy term insurance and invest the premium money saved in better vehicles than a life insurance policy.

ANNUITIES

An annuity is the only kind of life insurance policy that
really is *life* rather than *death* insurance. The only death
insurance aspect of an annuity is that it will pay beneficiaries if the annuity policyholder dies before the maturity of the policy. The main purpose of the policy is
to develop a tax-advantaged investment fund which pays
the holder after a specified number of years.

An annuity buyer purchases an insurance policy,
paying premiums periodically, in a single lump sum, or
in some periodic payment-lump sum combination. On
maturity, the policy pays its holder, usually a stated
amount, again periodically, in a lump sum, or both.
Taxation on investment gains is deferred until maturity.

Like whole-life policies, annuities have traditionally
been enormously profitable for life insurance companies
and huge sources of commissions for life insurance sellers. Also like whole-life policies, the net result for policyholders has been exactly the opposite. In periods of
considerable inflation, like the 1970s, the net loss to
policyholders in real dollars on annuity policies has been
enormous. Many annuity policies accreted value at as
little as 2–4 percent a year all during that period, while

inflation galloped ahead in double digits; those collecting on matured annuity policies therefore got far less in real dollars than they expected and needed. What is worse, these annuity policies have traditionally been purchased to fund retirement incomes. For many, the difference between what was expected and what was actually received in real dollars was the difference between reasonably comfortable later years and living at the edge of poverty.

In recent years, some insurance companies have, as with whole-life policies, begun to introduce higher-yielding annuities, in forms that maximize tax advantage. At this writing you can buy a standard annuity, which provides a fixed payout starting at a specified time, usually retirement, or the same kind of annuity in a flexible premium payment form, which allows great variation in the timing and amount of premium payments, thereby allowing you to take tax advantage of the money put into those payments. You can also buy an immediate annuity, which enables you to put a large lump sum into an annuity and then start taking payouts immediately thereafter. A single premium deferred annuity also takes a lump sum payment, but defers payout until a specified later time, with taxes on gain deferred until later and funds invested therefore accreting tax-free until payout. You can also fund an IRA with an annuity. Single premium deferred annuity yields are guaranteed yearly, with no penalty for taking your money out if yields in subsequent years go below the minimum rates specified when the original purchase is made. But you may have to pay a front load on purchase, or a back load—in effect, a penalty—for taking your money out within a specified time unless the yield drops below the guaranteed minimum rate.

THE QUESTION OF SAFETY

Traditionally, life insurance policies and annuities have been widely regarded as the safest kinds of investments. Actually, as investments, they have never been as safe as all that, although some policies—issued by large, well-known, tightly state-regulated national companies—have deserved their high reputations. But even when financial markets were not as volatile as they are today, many investors bought policies from shaky companies in states that regulated lightly and later found that the insurance proceeds they had been counting on were not there. Annuity funds all too often turned up severely depleted on maturity, and beneficiaries found themselves holding policies with death benefits that were not paid, often long after all premium payments had been completed. Texas was particularly notable for its scores of fly-by-night life insurance companies selling by mail across state lines. As a general practice, it is wise to buy insurance only from companies licensed to do business in your state. But if yours is a very lightly regulated state, then buy insurance only from nationally known, very large companies licensed to do business in states in which they are heavily regulated.

The money you put into an insurance company investment fund is not federally insured. Nor is it necessarily invested in the kinds of short-term obligations, many themselves federally insured, that compose money market mutual funds. There are reserves against losses required by law, and these are made quite large by the laws of some states, but there is in the long run nothing like the protection afforded by the Federal Deposit Insurance Corporation (FDIC). The money you put into a well-regulated insurance company's investment fund is as safe as the money you put into a sound blue-chip corporate bond, and that is relatively safe. But it is not catastrophe-proof, as insurance company ads and insurance sellers would have you believe.

In this period, there is considerable reason to believe that many insurance company investment funds are also not as safe as they were a decade or two ago. That is largely due to the operation of the new financial super-market, in which insurance companies compete with all other financial institutions for investors' money. That kind of competition makes for bigger promises and riskier investments on the part of some institutions. For ex-ample, the Baldwin-United failure of 1983 was a very large one, which involved both the promise of too-high interest on single premium deferred annuities and the use of insurance investment funds in other conglomerate activities. Many who had put some of their money into annuities—"safe" single premium deferred annuities—lost a good deal of that money when promised interest rates that seemed too good to be true turned out to be just that.

CHAPTER 11

Real Estate: A Classic Small Investor's Tool

When handled properly, real estate can be—and often is—one of the best possible kinds of investments. For scores of millions of people, at least since the end of World War II, it has certainly worked out that way.

There is really nothing quite like investing in real estate you know a good deal about. Your own home, a sound piece of residential or business property somewhere in your home area, or even some potential building lots out on the edge of your town or city—these can all be sources of long-term after-tax yield that is as good as or better than anything else you can put your money into. What you can get, if you handle it all carefully, is a combination of value growth, tax advantage, and leverage that are unbeatable.

Yes, leverage. It is built into the real estate purchasing transaction, because the cash you put in is usually only a smallish fraction of the purchase price, the rest being borrowed from financial institutions in the form of mortgages. There is nothing wrong with leverage, as long as it is built into a sound transaction. It is the feverish search for speculations into which you can put borrowed money that causes trouble.

Here is an example of how leverage has been working in favor of millions of American homeowners for the last several decades. Assume that you bought a home in a sound community for $40,000 in the mid-1960s, put down 20 percent, or $8,000, and took a $32,000 mortgage for the balance of the purchase price. Today, the market value of your house is likely to be somewhere around $200,000, which was a fairly normal increase for the period. But it is the value of the house that has quintupled; the value of your investment has grown far more than that. Assuming that your occupancy, with no rental being paid elsewhere, offsets your house payments, maintenance costs, and taxes—after figuring in the deductions on your interest and real estate taxes—what has happened is that your original $8,000 cash investment has grown to $200,000. That is a return of twenty-five times your investment—or 2,500 percent—for the whole period. Of course, you must figure in inflation, and your dollars are worth only about one third of what they were worth in the mid-1960s. Even so, you have in real dollars grown your money by about 800 percent. Whether 800 percent in real dollars or 2,500 percent in apparent dollars, you have done far better in your house than in most other kinds of investments during the period, and far more safely. If you had been in mutual funds or common stocks, you might have made nothing—or even lost money. If you had been in money market instruments of time certificates of deposit, you might have just about kept up with inflation—but you certainly would not have made 800 percent after figuring in inflation. You might have hit gold just right, buying at the low and selling at or near the high—that happened to some panic-stricken small investors, who were buying gold to hoard and found themselves rich quite by accident. But only your own home—if well located—could be counted on for that kind of return in that period. And on top of all that, you would, if you are fifty-five or older, today be entitled to a once-in-a-lifetime tax exemption on much of the gain; as of this writing, that exemption is $125,000. In this example, then, you would have bought at $40,000, had a gain of $160,000, and had to pay low capital gains taxes on only $35,000 of your gain. No matter how you look at it, for small investors home ownership has been, for some decades now, one of the main investing opportunities of a lifetime. For a very large number of families, that growth in the value of their own homes has been the only substantial store of value amassed in whole lifetimes of working, spending, saving, and investing.

RISING REAL ESTATE VALUES

The underlying fact is that since World War II the value of the bulk of American real estate, especially well-situated real estate, has grown enormously. Throughout the period, and even during the inflation-plagued 1970s and early 1980s, real estate values have consistently risen considerably faster than the rate of inflation.

That is a national tendency; there have certainly been significant exceptions to this pattern, and there will continue to be exceptions. As major cities slide rapidly downhill, much inner city land has lost a great deal of its value, becoming very nearly worthless. The blasted areas of New York City, such as Brownsville and portions of the South Bronx, are only the most spectacular examples of this; there are similar areas in many other major cities. There are also an increasing number of small cities and towns that have lost their main industries and are therefore very nearly ghost towns. Where that has occurred, people have had great difficulty selling their homes or businesses for anything at all, much less realizing anything near their previous values. Location has always been one of the keys to value in real estate; in uncertain times it becomes crucial.

Where homes and business properties have been reasonably well located, they have tended to grow far faster than the rate of inflation. Some businesses, especially farming businesses, have found that the appreciation in the value of their land, coupled with the steeply rising taxes that resulted when that land was in an expanding suburban or exurban area, literally forced them out of business, at huge profits. When land that was worth $500–$1,000 an acre rather suddenly becomes worth $10,000–$20,000 an acre, the taxes on that land often make doing a farming business on it far more expensive than the profits of the farm can possibly support. But the profits from the sale of land in that kind of situation have provided the basis for some considerable personal fortunes, especially since federal tax laws have provided some capital gains and inheritance tax relief. Given the fact that hundreds of thousands of farmers have been forced off the land in recent years because of high interest rates and low farm produce prices, the forced sale of suburban land at highly profitable prices was even more of a financial boon than it may have seemed at the time. Do be careful about investing in raw land, though. The promised superhighway may not come or may come a decade later than planned. So may the anticipated suburban residential and commercial development. If you buy raw land, you had best be prepared to hold it speculatively for a long time, paying taxes on it and making nothing on your money. Raw land is far more speculative than most other kinds of real estate investments.

In the rising real estate markets of the last two decades, even well-situated small business buildings and multiple dwellings proved profitable. That was very good for many small investors, who often added their own work—called *sweat equity*—to their money investments and created properties far more valuable than they had been when acquired.

However, any market rising as attractively as the residential real estate market did in that period inevitably invites speculation. Spurred by advisers who soberly stated that it was easy to make millions in real estate, thousands of small investors went far beyond prudent money and real estate management. They borrowed and bought as much and as fast as they could, upgraded and resold, took back second and third mortgages themselves when they couldn't get conventional financing, and altogether developed a greatly overheated residential real estate market, especially in such areas as California and portions of the Southwest. Then, when high interest rates and the unavailability of money suddenly made it impossible to continue to expand the bubble, it burst, with unsold properties and high interest on huge debts bankrupting many small speculators. Not their advisers, though; they counted their royalties and commissions and moved on to other advices and sales. *There is no free lunch in real estate investing, no foolproof way to make a million starting with next to nothing.* Those who tell you that you can usually know better.

There is a long-term rising market, however, and it can be used by small investors to make money, take tax advantage, and very profitably employ leverage—as long as they do not overreach or let investment professionals skim all or most of the profit off the top of the investment.

It is a rising market because the basic factors causing it to rise have remained the same for decades. At this writing, continuing very high interest rates, together with continuing very uncertain economic conditions and continuing and deepening technological unemployment, have stopped the development of anything like a boom in housing and other kinds of construction. And the truth is that nothing less than a massive housing boom would even begin to satisfy the pent-up housing demand of millions of Americans. The plain fact is that the national housing stock is aging, with many units—especially in the inner cities—becoming literally unfit for human habitation, even though people do live in them. It is equally plain that the national population continues to grow, slower than in some earlier periods but enough to create increased demand for housing. These are long-term factors; for decades, supply will diminish while demand grows, so the real estate market, in general, should continue to rise.

FAVORABLE TAX POLICY

Long-term national taxing policy also favors home and business property ownership. The concept of depreciation, as used in taxing policy, makes it possible to take large yearly tax deductions on income-producing property (except for farmland), fully or nearly fully depreciate that property for taxing purposes, change owners, and do it all over again, using the most recent sales price as the basis of the new round of tax deductions. Your accountant and some real estate professionals now call this kind of tax depreciation *accelerated cost recovery*, as that is the term used in the present tax law, but the principle has operated for some considerable time. This fast, repeated accelerated cost recovery or depreciation provides a huge tax shelter that has been an integral part of taxing policy and a motor in the real estate market for decades. It is even more of a tax shelter than it may seem, for it magnifies the leverage available from a real estate investment. When you use borrowed money, but take fast tax deductions based on the purchase price of a piece of real estate, your tax deductions may in the early years of the investment be larger than the amount of cash you actually put in. For example, if you put in 10 percent in cash and borrow the rest, and are in a combined 50 percent top tax bracket, you can save more than the cash you have put in on taxes within the first two years. Even if you are in a combined top 40 percent bracket, you can come out ahead in tax terms within the first three years. Those are enormously attractive figures, as long as you don't ruin the tax advantage by going into a bad real estate investment and having leverage work against you, as interest rates stay up and property values go down in a bad area, or find yourself victimized by professionals who take too much of the money in the investment for themselves, even short of actual fraud.

Always bear in mind that leverage can work in either direction and that no matter how good the times are when you buy, all may change far more quickly than you had anticipated. For small investors, who do not have the resources to ride out a storm, leverage can be particularly dangerous. A variable rate mortgage, for example, that moves up "no more than two points a year," can move up six points in six years, making it extraordinarily hard to meet mortgage payments on a home. A loan on business property, rolled over at the "going rate" shortly after interest rates have taken a big jump upward, may make an otherwise excellent piece of property impossible to carry, no matter how attractive the long-term prospects

and current tax advantages. As with so many other kinds
of investments, you can invest within a range running
from reasonable safety all the way to wildly unsafe speculation.

THE WAYS OF INVESTING
IN REAL ESTATE

There are several basic ways to invest in real estate. The
most widespread way of all is to buy and occupy your
own home. You can also trade in income-producing
properties of several kinds. Another way of participating
in ownership is as a limited partner, who buys a share
in a real estate venture. It is also possible to lend money
directly to real estate owners, as through direct placement
of second mortgage money, or to lend money through
others, as when you buy mortgages through mortgage
brokers or buy into large pools of mortgages through the
purchase of mortgage-backed securities.

For millions of small investors, real estate investment
starts and stops at home ownership. The best investment
of a lifetime may be a single family house, condominium,
or cooperative, located in a stable community that is
unlikely to be vulnerable to such disasters as urban decay,
single-industry-town plant closings, or the building of a
nuclear plant just over the next hill. Many people buy
that home, live in it or its equivalent in other places, sell
out with a big one-time tax break after they reach fifty-
five, and walk away with very large profits.

To take maximum advantage of the opportunity involved, the house must first of all be in a stable area,
preferably in an area that is well regarded for its schools

and cultural amenities, which much enhance home values. Aside from the economics of the matter, you and your family may greatly prefer to live in an area that does indeed have excellent schools and a good cultural life. However, it is wise to try to strike some sort of balance between living in that kind of area and the taxes you may have to pay to bring all that about. When a choice is available, the selection of a community with a wider tax base than that provided by residences alone is important, as is selection of a community with relatively large numbers of adults, rather than one swarming with children needing expensive educations. That the community has let in some industry can help enormously; those communities that have carefully kept out all or almost all industry tend to have either very high taxes or to have spent too little on education and culture. Those that have opted for very high tax rates may have succeeded in keeping real estate values very high, but in the process may have made it very difficult for people of modest means to hold on to their homes in those communities, as taxes and other costs have continued to rise.

A decade ago, it was wise to consider almost all center-city areas very skeptically, when it came to the home-buying decision. That is a little less so now, with *gentrification*, which is the move of some elements of the middle class back into some city areas. Add to that the government-assisted rehabilitation of some city areas, and it becomes apparent that there are some city neighborhoods that are relatively stable, and in which property values are rising at or even faster than national suburban norms. But even so, the main long-term trend is toward urban decay, in city after city right across the country. Our cities don't work very well, and the processes of decay accelerate, as city governments find themselves short of funds, face financial crises, are forced to cut back on essential services, and thereby contribute to the decay of their own cities. As long as the federal government does not make the rebuilding of America's cities a very high priority, the cities will continue to decay, for state and local governments have nowhere near the funds needed to reverse the long-term trends working here. And you cannot make sensible housing purchase and living decisions on the basis of the federal government's willingness to do what it has so far proved itself wholly unwilling to do. From an investment point of view, therefore, it is quite unwise to buy in the center cities, although there may be good buys in a few carefully selected neighborhoods in center cities and many neighborhoods on the outskirts of cities, where city and suburb essentially merge. Be careful even on city outskirts, though, for the crisis at the center of the city can mean wholly inadequate schools and city services there, too, which can greatly harm both the quality of life and the value of homes.

With all those cautions, the fact is that in many locations and in many parts of the country, real estate—and particularly the owner-occupied home—continues to be an excellent investment. In a period of long-term higher interest rates, your return on an investment may be smaller than it was in the 1970s and early 1980s, but it is still likely to compare very favorably with the return available from other kinds of investments.

SWEAT EQUITY

One classic way to invest in and profit greatly from real estate is to join your own work with the money you put into a property, with the resulting improvements greatly adding to the value of the property. The additional value coming from your work is often called *sweat equity*. There are people who all their working lives—and much beyond, into retirement—move into a series of houses, making improvements and building equity as they go. Some do it to improve living conditions, incidentally reaping large economic benefits later in life. Others do it as a matter of developing a part-time small business, taking profits as they go rather than plowing back profits into ever larger and more expensive homes. Either way, the net ultimate effect is similar—except that those who move into ever more expensive homes tend also to develop more expensive life-styles and by so doing partially negate the gains they make on their real estate. To use the growing value in a home to borrow money to pay for children's college educations may be necessary, and it may be wonderful to have the money there when you need it and can get it in no other way. But to spend money on conspicuous consumption and too-expensive college educations can merely waste the value in a house and other possible investment money besides.

Some small investors in real estate go beyond ownership of a single home and develop small-scale residential and business property holdings that can grow into sizable investments. For example, people who buy homes and businesses in depressed areas that are on their way back up can put a little money and a lot of sweat into properties, sell at substantial profits, and develop both capital and skills over the years. Excellent leverage can result from smallish cash investments and profitable sale after renovation; repeated again and again, sometimes for several properties at once, this technique can engender high profits. The other side of the coin, as always, is that leverage can work against you, as well. To use the profits of one sale to fund another purchase or even two more purchases, is reasonable—as long as your buys are right and your skills are good. But to pyramid credit upon credit, buying far too much too fast with the little actual cash you have, leaves you entirely vulnerable to such changes as rising interest rates, less available bank credit, less ability to pay on the part of mortgagees, fewer tenants than you anticipated, and a few bad guesses on your own part as to how fast property values will rise in a given area and how far they will go. With adequate starting cash, and good management skills, you stand a very good chance of making money with real estate you know in a sound area—as long as you handle the investment conservatively. But if you are undercapitalized or underskilled—or if you pay too much attention to those who tell you how to get rich quick—you can very easily lose your whole investment, if leverage goes against you.

LIMITED PARTNERSHIPS

You can also choose to own real estate as a partly owning "limited partner." Such a form goes beyond real estate; many other tax-sheltered investments, such as oil and gas ventures, also use the limited partnership form to gain maximum tax advantage with minimum risk for participating investors.

A limited partner buys a well-defined partnership share in a venture, investing a specific amount of money in return for a specified share in potential profits and limitation of losses up to the amount of money invested. By contrast, a general partner shares in profits and losses without limits, as all full partner-owners do. It is possible also to limit liability by making the investment as a corporation, with investors buying shares, but the tax advantages available from limited partnerships flow from the partnership form and would be lost if the corporate form were adopted. The device of the limited partnership makes it possible to take the full tax advantage; it also limits liability for limited partners, while passing partnership gains and losses through to the limited partners.

That has two very desirable results. In the early partnership years, when accelerated loss recovery and high interest payments on mortgages maximize losses, it passes those tax-deductible losses through to the limited partners, offering great tax advantage. In the later years of the partnership, it can pass through gains that will be taxed only once, rather than be subject to taxes on dividends and again on income, as occurs with corporation-generated income. In the early years, however, the tax advantages are of primary importance. It is the tax advantage that causes so many properties to be sold and resold after the early years.

The importance of the tax advantage makes the limited partnership form much more attractive to high-income investors than to small investors. However, a tax-advantaged real estate investment that is also a good business risk can be attractive to small investors, too— *as long, that is, as it is a good investment.* A bad investment, however wonderfully tax-advantaged, is still a bad investment.

For small investors and large investors alike, the main problem inherent in the limited partnership real estate investment is that, all too often, it is in real estate you know nothing at all about. These are usually quite large office buildings, housing projects, shopping malls, and the like far away, run by people and organizations you do not know and can in reality learn little about before you make your investment decision. In these situations, investors rely—perhaps too much—on those selling and sponsoring the investments. Sometimes that works out well, but a careful reading of the prospectus may also reveal that general partners and brokers may be taking a great deal of the possible profit off the top, before limited partners even begin to get their share. When that happens, the hazard is that so much may have been skimmed off that not enough will be left for limited partners to get their anticipated profits and their capital out in the long run. In the late 1960s and throughout the 1970s, limited partners in many real estate syndications found themselves facing huge losses when it became clear that their "profits" had been little more than early return of part of their own money and that, when it was time to return capital, the capital was no longer there. If you do go into a real estate limited partnership, let it be one that is selling portions of ownership in an area and in a specific investment you know something about or can learn enough about to make an informed decision. And never let the size of the tax advantage outweigh your sober assessment of the risks involved.

THE INVESTOR AS LENDER

One very traditional way of investing in the real estate market is as a lender of second mortgage money. That provides high interest at correspondingly high risk, especially when you participate in this market as a one-to-one lender, risking your limited investment money on individual second or even third mortgages.

Somewhat less risky is participation in the local second mortgage market as part of a group, the kind of group that often operates through a local lawyer, accountant, or real estate broker well known to all participants. By banding together, you are able to spread the risks somewhat, although in difficult times many second mortgage risks can go bad at once.

Both of these kinds of second mortgage participations have diminished considerably with the advent in recent years of a national second mortgage market, financed and guaranteed largely by federal government money. Now we are in the era of the *equity loan*—which is the old second mortgage, but now offered by major banks and other financial institutions rather than by groups of local investors and backed by government money and guarantees. Small investors can participate in these markets mainly by purchase of mutual funds, which have themselves purchased large denomination mortgage participation certificates and collateralized mortgage obligations (CMOs) from such private (but in effect government-backed) organizations as the Federal Home Mortgage Corporation (Freddie Mac). Small investors are increasingly being solicited for purchase of CMOs, which are at this writing being issued in smaller denominations. Where they are largely backed by federal guarantees, they may be reasonably safe investments and may continue to pay somewhat higher yields than Treasury securities. But they must be constantly compared for safety and yield with federally insured CDs.

Caution: Beware the high-paying uninsured second mortgage pool promoted by lightly regulated real estate brokers. Not long ago, as of this writing, many thousands of small investors in California and other Western states lost millions after listening to local mortgage speculators, who promised interest rates of as much as 25 percent per year on investments in second mortgages. The promoters,

riding a booming speculative market, took high placement fees from borrowers, spent a lot of money on pro-
motion, lured a lot of small investors, and then watched
as the housing market deflated and the investors lost their
money. There was a good deal of fraud involved, but the
main reason for the huge losses incurred was that—as
interest rates stayed high, instead of lowering as pre-
dicted—borrowers could not repay. And when they defaulted, those who had lent them money through brokers
lost a good deal. *There really is no Santa Claus; if high
returns had really been that sure and available, they would
have been snapped up by professionals before small investors ever got to them.*

Do consider real estate investment as a major possible
use of investment money, though. For people who take
the time to learn enough to make informed investment
decisions, real estate provides excellent opportunities.

CHAPTER 12

The All-Important Prospectus

Federal and state securities laws require that new issues of securities must be offered to prospective purchasers only by prospectus and that no seller can make any claims for an offering that are not fully covered in the prospectus. These laws go back to the Great Depression, when the country was in full recoil from what were seen then as the excesses of the speculative 1920s. Since then, the intent of the country, as expressed through its securities laws, has been to keep close control and regulation over those who issue and sell securities to the public, in an attempt to stamp out, or at least minimize, the widespread deception and often outright fraud that characterized earlier periods.

As a result, there is a constant small war in progress between securities issuers and federal and state regulatory bodies, with regulators for the most part successfully insisting that all the risks connected with each investment be very carefully spelled out in each prospectus. The skirmishes in that war take place mainly over *where* and *how* to state risks, rather than about the principle of stating the risks. The intent of the law has been very clear on the basic matter for several decades, through Republican

and Democratic, conservative and liberal administrations
on both federal and state levels.

It has been harder—much harder—to regulate selling behavior. For every securities seller who tells you
soberly to take the prospectus home, read it with care,
and then ask questions before investing, there are three
who tell you about the investment, give you the prospectus as an afterthought, and want you to invest right
now. There are also those who sell you over the phone
and then send you the prospectus afterward, only to cover
themselves legally. That is all understandable. The kinds
of commissions generated by small investors often scarcely
seem to justify the time it takes to do it right. But it is
not acceptable. You must fully understand an investment
before going into it, whether or not you have much real
help from its seller.

All this makes the prospectus an extraordinarily important document to understand, whether it is written
clearly or in difficult legal language. *The prospectus is
not just a piece of sales literature put together by a securities firm, to be used by securities sellers. It tells the
whole story of the investment and discloses the main risks
involved—sometimes a series of very damaging disclo-
sures. Such openness is forced upon issuers by regulatory
authorities. The prospectus is thus the most important
source of information you are likely to find on the security.*

Prospectus layouts differ, but you can be reasonably
sure that, if extraordinary risk factors have been identified
by regulators, that fact will appear right on the cover.
Then you will find, often in large black type, phrases
like "THIS OFFERING INVOLVES CERTAIN RISKS" and similar cautionary language. When you see something like
that on a prospectus cover, it is likely to be there only
because it has been forced on the issuer by the regulators,

or because the issuer knew that trouble could be expected if such a statement was not voluntarily placed there. *That kind of warning is meant to be a red flag, like the Surgeon-General's antismoking warning on a pack of cigarettes. If you ignore it, you are likely to do something very dangerous to your economic health.* At the very least, it should serve to alert you that there is real hazard here and cause you to read the prospectus—especially its section on risks—with extreme care.

Most prospectuses summarize the main elements of the offering first, with detailed backup information supplied later on. You should read that summary and reread it as necessary, noting any questions it raises. Use a separate sheet of paper rather than scribbling questions on the prospectus itself; otherwise, question builds on question, and all too soon questions, prospectus, and your own comments all merge into a very-difficult-to-read mass of type and handwriting. Many of your original questions will be answered as you go on from the summary to the main body of the prospectus. However, even after you have read and reread the whole prospectus, some questions may remain. That is when a discussion with a securities seller will prove fruitful.

After the summary will often come a listing of some of the risks involved, as negotiated by the issuer and regulators. Nothing in the list of risks is to be regarded as "standard" or "boilerplate." Everything stated as risk is to be taken very seriously and considered carefully. If you decide to make an investment, it should be only after understanding the risks involved. If you don't understand what some of the risk comments really mean, ask the seller, ask your accountant, ask other investors, and, if necessary, call the investor relations representative at the issuer's home office. Above all, don't under any circumstances shrug your shoulders and decide to take risks you do not understand because it is too much trouble to understand them. In truth, huge numbers of small investors do just that—and many of them lose their shirts.

Looking at the risks listed in the prospectus will raise all kinds of questions that are worth raising. For example, it may not have occurred to you on your own that a triple-tax-exempt bond fund offered to New York State residents may yield large rates of interest only because such a fund can't help but invest in certain extraordinarily risky New York City and New York State municipals— and probably in the equally risky bonds issued by such troubled New York State cities as Yonkers and Buffalo. Or the risk list of a new oil and gas exploration mutual fund may point out that the success of the fund can depend on very changeable factors entirely out of the control of the issuer, such as world oil and gas prices and production. And it may also indicate (1) that the whole thing is just a start-up operation, run by people with only so-so track records, who are going to go out with your money in hand to pick up oil and gas properties you will know nothing about, (2) that there will not be a ready resale market for the fund units, and (3) that under some circumstances you may lose your limited liability and possibly become liable for the general obligations of the whole enterprise (along with other limited partners, who— like you—may turn out to be not-so-limited partners). You can't rely on your securities seller to tell you all that and probably kill the sale; you must read and understand the risk list yourself. If, after reading all the red flags placed in the prospectus by the regulators, you still decide to invest, then that is your decision. It may indeed be a good one, but—good or bad—it will be an *informed* decision.

Beyond the summary and lists of risks will come the main body of the prospectus. The numbers relating to what the issuers and investment bankers get out of the issue before the remainder is applied to the purposes of the investment will tell you much about whether or not you want to invest. There are reasonable costs and fees to be expected; read enough prospectuses and go into enough investments, talk and read enough about investments, and you will begin to see who is milking the issue and who is taking reasonable costs and fees.

The section of the prospectus outlining management and its background is always of great significance. Look for who will actually be running an enterprise, rather than who sits on the board of directors. The most impressive-looking board of directors in the world may only testify as to the persuasive skills of the issuer. Your money will not be in the hands of directors, most of whom will have little to do with actual operations, but rather of those actually running things. A good-looking board of directors and an untried management team adds up only to an untried management team.

Be very sure that you study the financial statements at the back of the prospectus carefully, getting help from someone more experienced, such as an accountant, as necessary. Those financials will tell you a great deal, even by omission. For example, they will clearly indicate just how operational an issuer is; a company or fund with very small transaction numbers showing is probably, in reality, purely a start-up operation, which will use your money as—in essence—working capital. There is nothing particularly wrong with that, in and of itself, if you think the investment sound, but it is clearly something you must know. Similarly, the numbers relating to a going concern will tell you how the concern has been doing. For example, a mutual fund with considerable history may carry a ten-year investment performance graph, showing that a fund share was worth more ten years ago than it is today; that should—at the very least—raise serious questions as to whether or not you should invest in that fund. However, that part of the graph showing performance in recent years may convince you that this is an investment you want to make. That decision may be solidified by your study of the fund's investment choices, as indicated by the fund's current list of investments, also carried in the back of the prospectus.

The prospectus has a tremendous amount of valuable information to offer. Take the time to study it carefully. Such study can be a daunting task at the start of a "career" as a small investor, but learning to read a prospectus well is an indispensable skill for any investor, large or small.

How Money Can Grow

TABLE 1
YEARLY ASSET GROWTH ESTIMATE

Start of Year   Year-end   Change

Asset value
Savings accounts
  Short-term
  Long-term
Securities
  Stocks
  Bonds
  Other
Own business
Real estate
  Personal
  Business
Insurance
Pension and profit-sharing plans
Other
(gold, collectibles, etc.)
               Total

Debts
Mortgages
  Personal
  Business
Other business
Personal
               Total

Net apparent yearly asset growth
Impact of inflation
Net real asset growth

TABLE 2
CASH FLOW FORECAST

	Projected	Actual
Cash in		
Direct compensation		
(each full-time job, part-time job,		
or business salary separately)		
Dividends and interest		
(each source separately)		
Rental and royalities		
(each source separately)		
Alimony and child support		
Other*		
Total		
Cash out		
Mortgage repayments or rent		
Other fixed monthly payments		
Utilities (each separately)		
Taxes		
Insurance		
Alimony and child support		
Education		
Medical and dental		
Food		
Clothing		
Transportation		
Household maintenance		
Personal care		
Contributions		
Recreation		
Major purchases		
Other		
Total		
Net cash flow for month		
Net cumulative cash flow		
for year to date		

*Note: Possible additional sources of income this month (bonuses, gifts, sales of assets, second job not yet held, tax refunds, etc.)

TABLE 3
THE VALUE OF $1 OF PRINCIPAL, WITH COMPOUND INTEREST ACCUMULATED OVER 50 YEARS AT VARIOUS RATES

Interest Rate

Years	3%	6%	9%	12%	15%	18%
1	1.0300	1.0600	1.0900	1.1200	1.1500	1.1800
2	1.0609	1.1236	1.1881	1.2544	1.3225	1.3924
3	1.0927	1.1910	1.2950	1.4049	1.5209	1.6430
4	1.1255	1.2625	1.4116	1.5735	1.7490	1.9388
5	1.1593	1.3382	1.5386	1.7623	2.0114	2.2878
6	1.1941	1.4185	1.6771	1.9738	2.3131	2.6996
7	1.2299	1.5036	1.8280	2.2107	2.6600	3.1855
8	1.2668	1.5938	1.9926	2.4760	3.0590	3.7589
9	1.3048	1.6895	2.1719	2.7731	3.5179	4.4355
10	1.3439	1.7908	2.3674	3.1058	4.0456	5.2339
11	1.3842	1.8983	2.5804	3.4786	4.6524	6.1759
12	1.4258	2.0122	2.8127	3.8960	5.3503	7.2876
13	1.4685	2.1329	3.0658	4.3635	6.1528	8.5994
14	1.5126	2.2601	3.3417	4.8871	7.0757	10.1472
15	1.5570	2.3966	3.6425	5.4736	8.1371	11.9737
16	1.6047	2.5404	3.9703	6.1304	9.3576	14.1290
17	1.6528	2.6928	4.3276	6.8660	10.7613	16.6722
18	1.7024	2.8543	4.7171	7.6900	12.3755	19.6733
19	1.7535	3.0256	5.1417	8.6128	14.2318	23.2144
20	1.8061	3.2071	5.6044	9.6463	16.3665	27.3930
21	1.8603	3.3996	6.1088	10.8038	18.8215	32.3238
22	1.9161	3.6035	6.6586	12.1003	21.6447	38.1421
23	1.9736	3.8197	7.2579	13.5523	24.8915	45.0076
24	2.0328	4.0489	7.9111	15.1786	28.6252	53.1090
25	2.0938	4.2919	8.6231	17.0001	32.9190	62.6686

Interest Rate

Years	3%	6%	9%	12%	15%	18%
26	2.1566	4.5494	9.3992	19.0401	37.8568	73.9490
27	2.2213	4.8223	10.2451	21.3249	43.5353	87.2598
28	2.2879	5.1117	11.1671	23.8839	50.0656	102.9666
29	2.3566	5.4184	12.1722	26.7499	57.5755	121.5005
30	2.4273	5.7435	13.2677	29.9599	66.2118	143.3706
31	2.5001	6.0881	14.4618	33.5551	76.1435	169.1774
32	2.5751	6.4534	15.7633	37.5817	87.5651	199.6293
33	2.6523	6.8406	17.1820	42.0915	100.6998	235.5626
34	2.7319	7.2510	18.7284	47.1425	115.8048	277.9638
35	2.8139	7.6861	20.4140	52.7996	133.1755	327.9973
36	2.8983	8.1473	22.2512	59.1356	153.1519	387.0368
37	2.9852	8.6361	24.2538	66.2318	176.1246	456.7034
38	3.0748	9.1543	26.4367	74.1797	202.5433	538.9100
39	3.1670	9.7035	28.8160	83.0812	232.9248	635.9139
40	3.2620	10.2857	31.4094	93.0510	267.8636	750.3783
41	3.3599	10.9029	34.2363	104.2171	308.0431	885.4464
42	3.4607	11.5570	37.3175	116.7231	354.2495	1044.8268
43	3.5645	12.2505	40.6761	130.7299	407.3870	1232.8956
44	3.6715	12.9855	44.3370	146.4175	468.4950	1454.8168
45	3.7816	13.7646	48.3273	163.9876	538.7693	1716.6839
46	3.8950	14.5905	52.6767	183.6661	619.5847	2025.6870
47	4.0119	15.4659	57.4176	205.7061	712.5224	2390.3106
48	4.1323	16.3939	62.5852	230.3908	819.4007	2820.5665
49	4.2561	17.3775	68.2179	258.0377	942.3108	3328.2685
50	4.3839	18.4202	74.3575	289.0022	1083.6574	3927.3568

TABLE 4
THE VALUE OF $1 OF PRINCIPAL
TO WHICH $1 IS ADDED PER YEAR
WITH COMPOUND INTEREST
ACCUMULATED OVER 50 YEARS
AT VARIOUS RATES

Interest Rate

Years	3%	6%	9%	12%	15%	18%
1	1.0300	1.0600	1.0900	1.1200	1.1500	1.1800
2	2.0909	2.1836	2.2781	2.3744	2.4725	2.5724
3	3.1836	3.3746	3.5731	3.7793	3.9934	4.2154
4	4.3091	4.6371	4.9847	5.3528	5.7424	6.1542
5	5.4684	5.9753	6.5223	7.1152	7.7537	8.4420
6	6.6625	7.3938	8.2004	9.0890	10.0668	11.1415
7	7.8923	8.8975	10.0285	11.2997	12.7268	14.3270
8	9.1591	10.4913	12.0210	13.7757	15.7858	18.0859
9	10.4639	12.1809	14.1929	16.5487	19.3037	22.5213
10	11.8078	13.9717	16.5603	19.6546	23.3493	27.7551
11	13.1920	15.8700	19.1407	23.1331	28.0017	33.9311
12	14.6178	17.8821	21.9534	27.0291	33.3519	41.2187
13	16.0863	20.0151	25.0192	31.3926	39.5047	49.8180
14	17.5989	22.2760	28.3609	36.2797	46.5804	59.9653
15	19.1569	24.7825	32.0034	41.7533	54.7175	71.9390
16	20.7616	27.2129	35.9737	47.8837	64.0751	86.0680
17	22.4144	29.9057	40.3013	54.7497	74.8364	102.7403
18	24.1169	32.7600	45.0185	62.4397	87.2118	122.4135
19	25.8704	35.7856	50.1601	71.0524	101.4436	145.6290
20	27.6765	38.9927	55.7645	80.6987	117.8101	173.0210
21	29.5368	42.3923	61.8733	91.5026	136.6316	205.3448
22	31.4529	45.9958	68.5319	103.6029	158.2764	243.4868
23	33.4265	49.8156	75.7898	117.1552	183.1678	288.4945
24	35.4593	53.8645	83.7009	132.3339	211.7930	314.6035
25	37.5530	58.1564	92.3240	149.3339	244.7120	404.2721

Interest Rate

Years	3%	6%	9%	12%	15%	18%
26	39.7096	62.7058	101.7231	168.3740	282.5688	478.2211
27	41.9309	67.5281	111.9682	189.6989	326.1041	565.4809
28	44.2189	72.6398	123.1354	213.5828	376.1697	668.4475
29	46.5754	78.0582	135.3075	240.3327	433.7452	789.9480
30	49.0027	83.8017	148.5752	270.2926	499.9569	933.3186
31	51.5028	89.8898	163.0370	303.8477	576.1005	1102.4960
32	54.0778	96.3432	178.8003	341.4294	663.6655	1302.1252
33	56.7302	103.1838	195.9823	383.5210	764.3654	1537.6878
34	59.4621	110.4348	214.7108	430.6635	880.1702	1815.6516
35	62.2759	118.1209	235.1247	483.4631	1013.3457	2143.6489
36	65.1742	126.2681	257.3760	542.5987	1166.4975	2530.6857
37	68.1594	134.9042	281.6298	608.8305	1342.6222	2987.3891
38	71.2342	144.0584	308.0665	683.0102	1545.1655	3526.2991
39	74.4013	153.7620	336.8824	766.0914	1778.0903	4162.2130
40	77.6633	164.0477	368.2919	859.1424	2045.9538	4912.5913
41	81.0232	174.9506	402.5281	963.3595	2353.0069	5798.0378
42	84.4839	186.5076	439.8457	1080.0826	2708.2465	6842.8646
43	88.0484	198.7581	480.5218	1210.8125	3115.6334	8075.7602
44	91.7199	211.7437	524.8587	1357.2300	3584.1284	9530.5770
45	95.5015	225.5082	573.1860	1521.2176	4122.8977	11247.2610
46	99.3965	240.0987	625.8628	1704.8837	4742.4824	13272.9480
47	103.4084	255.5646	683.2804	1910.5898	5455.0047	15663.2580
48	107.5407	271.9585	745.8656	2140.9806	6274.4054	18453.8250
49	111.7969	289.3360	814.0836	2399.0182	7216.7162	21812.0930
50	116.1808	307.7561	888.4411	2688.0204	8300.3737	25739.4500

INDEX